What Today's Methodists Need to Know about John Wesley

Rem B. Edwards

Emeth Press
www.emethpress.com

What Today's Methodists Need to Know about John Wesley
Copyright © 2018 Rem. B. Edwards
Printed in the United States of America on acid-free paper

All rights reserved. No part of this book may be reproduced, or stored in a retrieval system or transmitted in any form or by any means, electronic, mechanical, photocopying, recording, scanning or otherwise, except as permitted by the 1976 United States Copyright Act, or with the prior written permission of Emeth Press. Requests for permission should be addressed to: Emeth Press, P. O. Box 23961, Lexington, KY 40523-3961. http://www.emethpress.com

Unless otherwise noted, quotations from John Wesley are from volumes of the Bicentennial Edition of *The Works of John Wesley*, Nashville, Abingdon Press, the first volume of which was published in 1984.

Library of Congress Cataloging-in-Publication Data

Names: Edwards, Rem Blanchard, author.
Title: What today's Methodists need to know about John Wesley / Rem B.
 Edwards.
Description: Lexington : Emeth Press, 2018.
Identifiers: LCCN 2018034028 | ISBN 9781609471316 (alk. paper)
Subjects: LCSH: Wesley, John, 1703-1791. | Methodist Church.
Classification: LCC BX8495.W5 E2575 2018 | DDC 287.092--dc23
LC record available at https://lccn.loc.gov/2018034028

Contents

PREFACE / v

CHAPTER ONE: WHAT DID WESLEY KNOW AND TELL? / 1
    WESLEY AS AN EVANGELIST / 1
    WESLEY AS WELL-INFORMED / 4
    LETTING OTHERS KNOW / 8

CHAPTER TWO: DON'T TAKE IT ALL LITERALLY / 15
    BEING CONTRARY TO EXPERIENCE / 16
    BEING CONTRARY TO REASON / 17
    OBVIOUSLY NON-LITERAL LANGUAGE / 19

CHAPTER THREE: DO TAKE IT ALL LOVINGLY / 23
    MORALLY UNCONSCIONABLE SCRIPTURES / 24
    UNLOVING SCRIPTURES THAT CONFLICT WITH
        LOVING SCRIPTURES / 30

CHAPTER FOUR: POOR FAITH: BELIEFS WITHOUT WORKS AND LOVE / 35
    POOR FAITH AS MENTAL ASSENT TO THE DOCTRINES OF
        CHRISTIAN ORTHODOXY / 35
    DOCTRINAL FAITH ALONE / 38

CHAPTER FIVE: GOOD FAITH THAT WORKS BY LOVE / 43
    THE FAITH THAT WORKS / 43
    THE FAITH THAT WORKS THROUGH LOVE / 44
    WESLEY'S OWN LOVING WORKS / 46
    THE FAITH THAT GROWS: SALVATION AND SANCTIFICATION / 51

CHAPTER SIX: OTHER CHRISTIANS AND OTHER FAITHS / 57
    DIVERSE CHRISTIAN PRACTICES 57

DIVERSE CHRISTIAN BELIEFS / 58
　　NON-CHRISTIAN BELIEFS AND PRACTICES / 61

CHAPTER SEVEN: PEOPLE AND ANIMALS IN THE IMAGE OF GOD / 67
　　PEOPLE IN THE IMAGE OF GOD / 67
　　ANIMALS IN THE IMAGE OF GOD / 71

CHAPTER EIGHT: THE GOODNESS OF GOD / 81
　　GOD'S POWER / 82
　　GOD'S FEELINGS, LOVE, AND COMPASSION / 86
　　GOD'S PRESENCE / 90

CHAPTER NINE: MEANS AND ENDS / 97
　　CONFUSING MEANS AND ENDS / 98
　　THE MEANS AND ENDS OF GRACE / 101
　　FINAL ENDS / 105

CHAPTER TEN: WAS JESUS EVER HAPPY? ARE YOU? / 111
　　WHAT DID WESLEY MEAN BY "HAPPINESS"? / 111
　　A WESLEYAN ARGUMENT FOR THE HAPPINESS OF JESUS / 113
　　LOVE AND OBEDIENCE TO THE LOVE COMMANDMENTS / 114
　　SPIRITUAL BELIEFS, KNOWLEDGE, EXPERIENCES,
　　　　DISPOSITIONS, VIRTUES, AND ACTIVITIES / 116
　　MORAL BELIEFS, KNOWLEDGE, EXPERIENCES,
　　　　DISPOSITIONS, VIRTUES, SENSITIVITIES, AND ACTIVITIES / 117
　　PLEASURES, ENJOYMENTS, JOY / 118
　　FREEDOM FROM AS MUCH PAIN, SUFFERING, LOSS,
　　　　AND UNHAPPINESS AS HUMANLY POSSIBLE / 120

ABOUT THE AUTHOR / 127

Preface

Most ordinary Methodists and other Wesleyans need and want to know much more than they do about John Wesley. They just don't realize it yet!

I discovered this by teaching Wesley to a number of adult Sunday school classes at Church Street United Methodist Church in Knoxville, TN during the past several years.

This book will get you underway in studying Wesley. It will not finish the job. You will still have a lot to learn after you read it, but by then you can decide for yourself if you want to go any further. Studying and discussing Wesley with others in Sunday school classes or discussion groups would be greatly beneficial to you.

Most of us need to understand why we are and wish to remain Methodists or other Wesleyans. We have many personal reasons for this, but if we learn enough about John Wesley, we will see that one of the best reasons is that he got us off to a really good start. He showed us how to be sane, well informed, intellectually honest, scripturally informed, socially engaged, and deeply spiritual members of the living body of Christ. Our task now is to sustain and develop what he started.

John Wesley was an incredible person both in what he did and what he thought. Viewed against the background of the Christian scholars of his day and those who went before him, his thinking was immensely creative, insightful, and at times downright radical. From this book you will learn more about what he thought than about what he did, but both will be explored. Most of us know a little bit about *what he did*, but we know almost nothing about *what he thought*. We know that he founded the Methodist Church, that he was impressed by the Moravians during storms at sea, and that he was a revival preacher. But what else?

Very few Wesleyans know very much about Wesley's ideas. When you find out about them, you may be both astonished and very pleasantly surprised. So much of what he had to say is as fresh and relevant to us today as it was to so many others during his own lifetime. Wesley can enlighten us now. This book may allow Wesley to switch a light on for you. Have you ever read anything actually written by Wesley? Very few Wesleyans today have ever read any of his own words. By the time you finish this book, you will have, and you may be quite amazed by what he had to say. Sadly, very few of our ministers ever tell us very much about Wesley himself, or about our distinctive Wesleyan theological heritage. Very few ever quote Wesley in their sermons or tell us that he had anything to say that is worth knowing or reading, but this book will provide many wonderful quotes from Wesley for both sermonizing and meditation purposes.

If our Wesleyan church staffs and members really understood Wesley and what he has to offer to us now, maybe our churches would once again flourish and grow. Wesley was as much concerned with abundant life in this world as in the next. The lives we have now really matter to us, to others, and to God, he insisted. He preached and wrote profusely to help us "get to heaven"—but also to help make this world "almost Heaven on earth." He affirmed God's kingdom on earth as it is in heaven. He wanted the poor, uneducated, laboring, downtrodden, and forgotten people—the ones who became the first Methodists—to live meaningful, worthwhile, fulfilled, happy, loving, helpful, and abundant lives both here and now and hereafter. He would have the same concerns for everyone today. For all our progress and prosperity, many people now seem to be living meaningless, empty, unfulfilled, unhappy, unloving, distressed, hurtful, and vacuous lives. Wesley can show us how to live more abundant lives, happier lives, more fulfilled and meaningful lives. This book explains how he worked it all out. Perhaps it will enable you to work such things out for yourself.

I do not agree with Wesley about everything, and you will not either. Wesley did not even agree with himself about everything! He often changed his own mind in light of better information, deeper thought, and more experience. To keep track of this, many scholars distinguish between the early, middle, and late or "mature" Wesley. This book concentrates mainly on the most mature, or perhaps the most plausible, Wesley. It ignores many of his obsolete and indefensible ideas. For example, Wesley mistakenly associated democracy with lawlessness. He was a Tory who opposed the American Revolution and democracy itself in favor of the divine right of kings—biblically based, of course.[1] We would not want to accept or defend that! What exactly counts as indefensible or obsolete is always a matter of judgment. After reading this book, your overall judgment about Wesley is likely to be very positive.

Seen against the background of the Christian thinkers who came before him, Wesley's vision for Christian living, doing, thinking, seeking, choosing, believing, loving, helping, and growing is still immensely creative, insightful, and appealing. Seen against his historical background, some of his Christian insights were downright revolutionary and revelatory. You may not know that yet. You will by the time you finish this book!

The basic themes in chapters two and three were developed in my article titled "John Wesley's Non-Literal Literalism and Hermeneutics of Love," published in the Fall, 2016 issue of the *Wesleyan Theological Journal*. The last chapter is a modified version of my article titled "Was Jesus Ever Happy? How John Wesley Could Have Answered," published in the Fall, 2017 issue of the *Wesleyan Theological Journal*. Many thanks to Abingdon Press, Nashville, TN, for permission to use the quotes from the Bicentennial Edition of *The Works of John Wesley*.

Notes

1. John Wesley, *Some Observations on Liberty*, London: R Hawes, 1776.

CHAPTER 1

WHAT DID WESLEY KNOW AND TELL?

Sometimes preachers exaggerate, even Methodist preachers, even John Wesley. He once wrote that he was "a man of one book," and that "I want to know one thing, the way to heaven—how to land safe on that happy shore."[1] The Bible was indeed his "number one" book, but it definitely was not his "one and only" book. He had an insatiable curiosity about almost everything, not just about the way to Heaven and how to get there, and not just about the Bible. He was one of the most learned, intellectually honest, well-informed, well-read, and theologically insightful persons of his own time and place. He was familiar with practically everything that was going on in the intellectual world of his day. Yet, he spent almost all of his professional career working as a traveling evangelist, an itinerant preacher. How was it possible for him to become so well informed?

Wesley as an Evangelist

Wesley was not a professional College Teacher—not for long. He was not a Divinity School Theologian. He did not write a book on Systematic Theology. He preached and wrote the good news of Christianity as plain truth, in plain language, for plain people. He expected all Methodist preachers to do this. He expected and encouraged all of his ministers to be well-educated, but not to be fancy "show offs." As he put it, they should abstain "from even the show of learning."[2]

Wesley was not a professional scholar, but he was still a very serious and accomplished scholar. For a short time, he actually did some college teaching or tutoring. As a very young man, and before he sailed off to Georgia to preach to the Indians (with whom he never had any significant contact or success), he taught or tutored in logic, philosophy, and Greek while he was a Fellow at Oxford University. For the rest of his life, he continued to read and study deeply and extensively. Yet, for most of his life, he was a traveling revival preacher, one who unintentionally founded a new and very large protestant church, the Methodist Church, now with many Wesleyan branches. How did it happen?

Today Wesley is known mainly as the founder of the Methodist Church. How did it get started? To make a long story very short, in 1738 one of his friends, George Whitefield, a late-comer to Wesley's Holy Club at Oxford, started preaching out in the open fields to huge crowds of poor and mostly uneducated people. These people were not being reached by and seldom if ever attended the mostly upper-class established (state supported) Church of England. Whitefield's spectacular field preaching was very successful, and he made many converts. He invited John and Charles Wesley to try it.

As ordained, prim, and proper Anglican priests, at first they were very reluctant to do field preaching, but once they tried it, they found that it worked exceptionally well for them also. The Wesleys, Whitefield, and others who joined their evangelistic crusade started a sweeping revival movement that quickly spread through the British Isles and the American Colonies. This was and is called the "Great Awakening." In England, it was largely a Methodist Awakening. It peaked during the early 1740s, but for many decades after that, Wesley and his associates traveled all over England conducting revivals and establishing new congregations. They often faced local opposition from resident Anglican ministers and from angry and sometimes violent mobs. Whitefield carried the Great Awakening to the American Colonies, though significant anticipations of it were already there before he arrived.

John Wesley lived to be a fairly old man. He was 88 years old when he died. He was born in 1703 and died in 1791. Between 1740 and 1790, he spent much of his time on horseback or in horse-drawn carriages riding from one city and village to another throughout the British Isles conducting revival meetings and start up new congregations. (He did not have much success in Presbyterian Scotland.)

Wesley was not a "fly by night" evangelist who came to town, saved a lot of souls, moved on, and then a month later everyone was right back where they started. No, John and Charles Wesley were accomplished organizers, John especially. Earlier, he and his friends in the Oxford Holy Club were so methodical in their devotional and public service activities that people made fun of them. They were called "Methodists" in derision. At first this was a silly and offensive label. John eventually decided that he liked it, and it stuck. "Methodical" was very descriptive of John's organizational work following his revivals.

In the many cities, towns, and counties where the Wesleys preached, hundreds and often thousands of new converts responded positively to their sermons, hymns, prayers, and services. They and their supporters arranged follow-up care in order to sustain their ongoing spiritual and moral nurture. Somehow, capable local leaders were found wherever they went. New converts were organized into larger and smaller societies, bands, and classes. Members of these supportive communities kept in close contact with one another, and they helped and nurtured one another spiritually, socially, financially, and educationally. Rules for belonging and proper living were strict. Personal imperfections were openly discussed so they could be corrected. The small classes were groups of a dozen or so people who lived close together, could meet once or more a week, and could be visited occasionally by their leaders. Lay leaders emerged more or less spontaneously within these groups, and many of them were women. Many evolved into lay preachers.

The larger local groups were called "societies"—Methodist societies. They were not called "churches," and their "meeting houses" or "preaching houses" were not called "church buildings." The buildings they built or bought were in fact churches, but John and Charles Wesley did not intend to create a new protestant church or separate denomination, Charles especially. That ultimately happened, thanks largely to the American Revolution, but the Wesleys always insisted that Methodism was only a reform movement within the larger established Church of England. Many other reform groups already existed, so this was nothing new.

The Methodist movement grew rapidly, mostly among the lower laboring classes of British society and the American Colonies. By the time John Wesley died, there were around 72,000 members in the British Isles and 60,000 in the by-then independent America. Most early Methodists were commoners and very ordinary people. Most were unchurched, uneducated, poor, illiterate, neglected, indebted, and often destitute. They were coal miners, factory workers, housewives, household servants, farmers, and so on. Some were unemployed. Most worked for very low wages in the factories and mines of the developing Industrial Revolution. In that highly social-class-conscious English society, upper class Anglican Church members and priests did not want to mix with such "low down" people or to minister to them. Most Anglican priests did not know or care about the desperate social conditions under which they were living. Most would not allow John Wesley to preach from their pulpits, so the world became his parish.

Most early Methodists were among "the least of these," as Jesus would have said. Wesley convinced them that they were somehow just as good as the "greatest of these"—as the world measures greatness. They were equally as worthy of salvation, and equally as valuable in and to themselves and in the eyes of God as members of the upper crusts of British society. Lords, ladies, gentlemen, and prosperous middle class commoners regarded them as their inferiors—and themselves as their obvious superiors. They were definitely not up to being their equals. Members of the upper classes resented, resisted, and even feared John Wesley. Despite his dedicated Toryism and his fierce opposition to democracy, they saw him as a "leveler" and "equalizer" because he preached that everyone is equally a sinner, equally loved by God, and equally as valuable intrinsically, that is, in, to, and for themselves. Most important of all, Christ came to save everyone equally, literally everyone. Wesley's Tory politics did not harmonize very well with his most mature moral and spiritual convictions.

Jesus himself identified intensely with "the least of these." When you help such people, "You have done it unto me," he said (Matthew 25:40). When at his best, Wesley also identified indiscriminately and intensely with everyone. So should we. Of course, Wesley was not always at his best. Neither are we.

Wesley as Well-informed

Believe it or not, a very direct connection exists between Wesley as an itinerant evangelist and his being one of the best informed and most thoughtful persons of his day. Over the course of fifty years or more, Wesley rode at least 250,000 miles all over the British Isles, going from one revival to the next. For decades, he traveled mostly on horseback, but in the 1770s he began to ride in a horse-drawn carriage. He could make 50 to 60 miles per day on horseback. His longest ride was 90 miles in about 20 hours. That was a long day! He was firmly convinced of the health benefits of horseback riding.

What did Wesley do with himself while riding from one revival site to the next? Did he just sit on his horse and enjoy the scenery? No, he put his riding time to very good use. Do you think you could read a book, or many books, while riding a horse? Well, Wesley could and did! He read numerous books while riding from place to place. Beyond his years at Oxford, this is how he found time to become one of the most learned and well-read scholars of his day. Familiar paintings and statues show him riding his horse with a book in hand. That book wasn't the Bible. Wesley said he read books on philosophy, history, and poetry while he rode. He also read many of the most important religion and theology books written through the centuries and during his lifetime.

A very distinguished Wesley scholar, Albert Outler, said that John Wesley recognized four sources of religious knowledge—scripture, reason, tradition, and experience, scripture being the most fundamental. Maybe there were more—conscience, for example. In theory, conscience, as Wesley understood it, was covered by "experience," that is, by the experiences of our "moral sense." For emphasis, however, in later pages it will be considered separately.

For Wesley, scripture came first in theory but not always in practice and application. Ideally, all of these sources of moral and religious insight work in harmony—with considerable help from the grace of God. Wesley was exceptionally well informed about and competent in all of them. The weakest element in this "quadrilateral," as Outler called it, is "tradition." There are many and diverse traditions within Christendom. Choices must be made among them. Just what counts as "that old time religion" varies significantly within groups and between denominations. Wesley especially emphasized the earliest Christians and church fathers.

Wesley could read the Bible in Greek, Hebrew, and English. Critical biblical scholarship had made some but not much progress in his day. Wesley had his own profound ideas about how to interpret the scriptures, as you will soon see. He was also well versed in philosophical thinking. He carefully studied many ancient philosophers like Socrates, Plato, and Aristotle, and many modern philosophers like Descartes, Bacon, Leibnitz, Locke, and others. He was mindful of the great diversity of historical Christian theology and practices. He especially admired, respected, and commended the earliest Christian thinkers. He read Luther, Calvin, and the prominent Anglican and Deistic thinkers of his day. He agreed with some of them and disagreed with others. He always thought deeply and carefully. So should we. He set many good examples for us.

Wesley had an immense curiosity about the Christian gospel and almost everything else, including what we would call the "natural sciences." He eagerly learned and accepted what the best scientists of his day were saying. He thought that an accurate understanding of the universe would please, serve, and glorify God, its Creator. He did not fear science or the advance of human knowledge. He lived long before Charles Darwin, but he fully embraced the very best natural science of his day.

In Wesley's day, "natural science" wasn't called that. It was called "natural philosophy." The natural sciences as we know them were then regarded as parts of philosophy. They had not developed enough subject matter or methodology to drop off of philosophy, their parent tree. No one at that time could go to a university and sign up for courses in physics, chemistry, biology, paleontology, astronomy, or geology as we know them. But they could study natural philosophy.

Some scientific disciplines like physics (Sir Isaac Newton) and astronomy (Copernicus and Galileo) had made significant strides toward independence. Wesley studied and embraced the best science of his day. He published lengthy books about it, and he often updated, revised, and republished them. He heavily edited several works on natural philosophy written by others and then republished them in his own name. Unlike Luther and Calvin, Wesley accepted the Copernican view that the sun, not the earth, is the center of our solar system, and that our earth revolves around it once a year and turns on its axis every 24 hours. He rejected the Biblical and Ptolemaic picture of the earth as the flat center of a very small three-story universe, undergirded by water (or fire), and encircled by the heavens above with their fixed and wandering stars.

In his day nothing had happened in biology, geology, or paleontology to shake his faith in the literal truth of the Genesis creation story, or his assumption that we live in a relatively small Copernican universe of fairly recent origins. The universe was 6000 years old according to Bishop Usher.[3] It was only 4000 years old according to Sir Isaac Newton.[4] Wesley allude to both numbers in different writings. That was good enough and close enough for him *and for the very best "scientific" minds of his day*. Nobody then knew any better. Current estimates are that our universe is around 13.7 billion years old. No one in his day anticipated anything like that.

Commenting on astronomy and "those scriptural expressions which seem to contradict the earth's motion," Wesley *may* have written, "This general answer may be made to them all, that, the scriptures were never intended to instruct us in philosophy, or astronomy; and therefore, on those subjects, expressions are not always to be taken in the literal sense, but for the most part, as accommodated to the common apprehension of mankind."[5] Wesley may not have written this and it was added by a later editor, but it certainly expresses Wesley's perspective. He embraced the best natural science of his day and was not intimidated by it, and this is highly significant for us here and now. He would encourage us now to be open to the very best of today's natural sciences and philosophies, though none of these speak with one voice about everything. He was confident that even scientific truth would set us free.

The relatively primitive state of the natural sciences in his day is well illustrated by Wesley's viewpoint on the basic elements of chemistry; there were only four, Earth, Air, Fire, and Water. Wesley often wrote about these. This chemistry dates back to a very early pre-Socratic Greek philosopher named Empedocles. By the time Wesley came along, almost everyone except maybe Robert Boyle still believed that there were only these four basic chemical elements. Wesley himself was fascinated by electricity, and he suspected that it might be a fifth element. As we will see, he pioneered therapeutic uses of electricity for both physical and mental afflictions.

So, when Wesley said that he was reading "philosophy" while riding his horse, much of that was natural philosophy, the early stages of today's natural sciences.

Letting Others Know

Wesley highly valued human knowledge, truth, and honest inquiry for himself, for others, and for the Glory of God. Echoing Aristotle, he claimed, "The desire of knowledge is an universal principle in man, fixed in his inmost nature."[1] He added, "Knowledge is an excellent gift of God, particularly knowledge of the Holy Scriptures."[2] He did not stop there, however. He was cautious about how far we could expect to get in trying to understand the created universe. "How small a part of this great work of God is man able to understand," he wrote, "But it is our duty to contemplate what he has wrought, and to understand as much of it as we are able."[3]

It is also our Christian duty to share what we have learned with others. Let's take a look at some of the things Wesley did and said to spread human knowledge to others—for the Glory of God, for the benefit of ourselves and humankind, and to satisfy his own "desire of knowledge." Wesley was an inquisitive, bounteous, and fruitful reader, communicator, writer, editor, and publisher. He was eager to let others in on what he had learned, but he did not write or publish for an academic audience. He wrote mainly for ordinary people, but especially for the lay ministers who contributed so significantly to the growth of the Methodist movement. Abingdon Press, today's Methodist Publishing House in Nashville, TN, began to publish the definitive Bicentennial Edition of *The Works of John Wesley* in 1984. The project is far from finished in 2018. His writings will fill around thirty three volumes, all thick and heavy, each around 500 to 700 pages in length. Only twenty some odd volumes have been published thus far. Wesley was one of the most prolific published authors of his century.

There is a real puzzle about how and when Wesley found enough time to do all the reading he did. "On horseback" is the answer. There is an even greater puzzle about when he found time to write all the books, sermons, essays, instructions, letters, and journal entries that he wrote. He probably could not write with a quill pen while riding on horseback. He did some writing at night and between sermons. After he started riding in a horse-drawn carriage rather than on horseback, Wesley took a small writing table and many books along with him as he traveled. Much of his writing must have been done during the coldest months of winter when he could not ride circuits had to stay put in London.

Wesley believed very strongly in educating adults, children, and his lay ministers. And he did something about it. He was a modernist who did not fear the advance of science and human knowledge. He welcomed it. He insisted upon it. He relished and debated tough questions. He was convinced that God gave us minds and expects us to use them. We should love God with all our minds as well as with all our souls, hearts, and strength. We should have "the mind of Christ," as St. Paul put it, and we should "*prove* what is that good, and acceptable, and perfect will of God" (Romans 12:2; italics added). Wesley wanted to make the very best and latest human knowledge available to everyone, especially his Methodists. Illiterate Methodist adults were taught reading, writing, arithmetic, and much else for their own good both in this world and the next.

Wesley's classes, bands, societies, Sunday schools, and schools for children did far more than nurture hearts, minds, and souls spiritually. They empowered the people called Methodists to read their Bibles along with many other religious writings and practical self-help books. They enabled them to manage their everyday health, business, and practical affairs more efficiently, and they learned how to calculate so they could gain, save, and give all the money and wealth they could.

Where did Wesley get all the new preachers needed to serve the many new Methodist societies (alias churches) being established in cities and towns throughout the land? Some ministers served only one church—local preachers. Others served several churches—circuit riders. "Methodist Connexion" preachers met together with Wesley once a year in Annual Conferences. But where did they come from? Very few ordained Church of England ministers ever associated with the Methodist movement, despite decades of Wesley's effort to recruit them. Most early Methodist ministers were unordained lay preachers who started out with very little education or theological training.

Because most early Methodist preachers were unordained, they could not administer the sacraments of communion and baptism. Still, the Wesleys strongly commended, and many members greatly desired, frequent participation in communion services. For decades, how to resolve this conflict was one of Methodism's most serious and hotly debated doctrinal and practical problems. Sending Methodists to nearby Anglican Churches for communion did not prove to be a very practical or desirable solution.

As long as they remained within the Church of England, Wesley and his ministers were stuck with "apostolic succession." This meant that ministers could be ordained only by Bishops who, at least in theory, could trace their own ordination back to St. Peter himself or to one of the other original apostles. After the American Revolution, Wesley himself, who was not a Bishop, ordained Thomas Coke as a Superintendent for the American churches. He authorized Coke to cross the Atlantic and ordain Francis Asbury as another Superintendent. In turn, Asbury could then further ordain many American lay ministers and empower them to administer the sacraments. Asbury himself was a largely self-educated lay minister. He was also a remarkably successful itinerant evangelist who earlier came to the Colonies from England. Unlike the colonial Anglican priests, he remained in America during the Revolutionary War. Ordaining him with the authority to ordain others was Methodism's decisive break with Anglicanism. Reluctantly, John took this step it as a matter of practical necessity. Charles resisted it to the end. Against John Wesley's wishes, American Methodists called their Superintendents "Bishops." They thought that if it looks, walks, acts, and quacks like a Bishop, it really is a Bishop!

Lay preachers emerged gradually and somewhat miraculously from their local Methodist communities, classes, bands, and societies. Some members were much more vocal and natural leaders than others. Some began to preach. Some lay preachers served churches while holding their regular jobs during the week. Others became full time local preachers or circuit riders. Almost all were poorly educated at first, especially in theology, and they begged Wesley to tell them what to read and how to preach. He obliged. His published sermons and other writings spelled out the basic doctrines and practices that Methodists were expected to take most seriously. Wesleyans today should know much more than they do about his sermons and the theology developed and expressed in them. Future chapters of this book will draw heavily upon them.

Wesley preached countless times over the years. He also wrote and published numerous pamphlets, tracts, sermons, directives, policies, and books. His publications guided the lay preachers who served the local

Methodist societies or congregations. One hundred and fifty one of his authentic sermons have survived. They were republished by Abingdon Press in the first four volumes of the Bicentennial Edition of his *Works*. The very best of his spoken preaching was refined and published in his thoughtful and carefully organized written sermons. Wesley never wrote an academic book on Systematic Theology, but he produced one of the most insightful Christian theologies ever written in his many published sermons. If you are not yet convinced that Wesley was a great theologian, please keep on reading!

In the early 1740s, John Wesley began to publish pamphlets, tracts, sermons, essays, letters, and instructions for his "Methodist Connexion" preachers and society members. He continually revised, published, and republished such materials. For decades, he added more and more carefully crafted sermons until very close to his death in 1791. In 1778, he began publishing the *Armenian Magazine*. It contained additional sermons, religious reading materials, and the latest news about the Methodist movement. It was something like the *Christian Century* of its day.

As more and more Methodist lay persons and preachers were enabled and encouraged to read and study, Wesley republished writings by other authors. He established a serious and profitable publishing business in the 1740s. In effect, he created the first Methodist Publishing House. Around 1750, he republished 50 carefully edited books by other authors in his *Christian Library*. Most were theological, but others were more generally informative, helpful, and practical.

In Wesley's day, there were no strict copyright laws. Anyone could republish someone else's book with their own name on the cover as its author. Wesley did this himself. Though first written by others, he gave his own name as the author of many of the 50 books in his Christian Library. He did not always give credit to the original author. He heavily edited everything to suit himself. He shortened most of these books so they could be printed and sold more cheaply. His method for abridged them was to cut out the ideas, words, sections, and pages that he disagreed with. He often added his own explanatory words, sentences, paragraphs, and whole sections. He printed these books as cheaply as possible so even poor Methodists and others could afford to buy them. To save money, most did not have hard covers. They were printed as paperback books. John Wesley was the father of paperback books!

Wesley designed a program of study for his lay ministers and for others better educated. It was addressed to "the Clergy of our own Church" (the established Church of England), but it was applicable, he said, to all ministers "of whatsoever denomination." Very few of his "Methodist Connexion" lay ministers ever fully met Wesley's high educational standards.

In this 1756 "Address to the Clergy," Wesley distinguished between the natural and the acquired gifts of ministers. Among the *natural gifts* were, first, "a good understanding, a clear apprehension, a sound judgment, and a capacity of reasoning with some closeness."[6] Next was "liveliness and readiness of thought" so that ministers could "answer a fool according to his folly." "A good memory"[7] was desirable so they could keep track of everything. All of these natural gifts needed further development to become acquired intellectual virtues.

The desirable *acquired gifts* of ministers required a lot of effort and work. These were a competent knowledge:

- of the duties of their own office,
- of the scriptures, including their "original tongues,"
- of "profane history, likewise, of ancient customs, of chronology and geography"—all essential for interpreting and understanding the scriptures,
- of "the sciences" including logic, the art of "apprehending things clearly, judging truly, and reasoning conclusively."[8]

Recall that Wesley earlier taught Logic at Oxford. In 1756 he translated and then republished in his own name a logic textbook, *A Compendium of Logic,* to be used by his lay ministers and others so they could learn to think more clearly and rationally. Ideally, ministers also needed to know:

- metaphysics, the general philosophical theory of reality or being,
- natural philosophy, the beginnings of what we today call the "natural sciences,"
- geometry, because it forms habits of clear and logical thinking,
- the early Church Fathers, "the most authentic commentators on Scripture,"

- later Christian thinkers,
- "the world, a knowledge of men, of their maxims, tempers, and manners, such as they occur in real life."
- Prudence or common sense, the ability to adapt behavior to existing circumstances, was important, as were "good breeding," and
- a "strong, clear, musical voice, and a good delivery."[9]

Wesley expected far more of his ministers than their intellectual development and practical talents. The actual *value* of all their intellectual and practical gifts was "little in comparison" with the immense significance of additional spiritual and moral gifts. The most essential of these for a ministerial "steward of the mysteries of God" were practical efforts "to *glorify* God and to save souls," and an inner love to God and neighbors "to a degree beyond that of ordinary Christians."[10] Ministers with Divinity School degrees today would do well to meet Wesley's high educational, moral, and spiritual standards!

To what extent did Wesley actually enforce his high educational standards? He was more inclined instead to enforce his moral, spiritual, practical, and doctrinal standards. Over the decades, Wesley exercised almost absolute authority over the ministers who were a part of his "Methodist Connexion." He often purged or excluded lay ministers if they were morally defective, if they were poor speakers, communicators, and administrators, if they pushed too hard for immediate separation from the established Church of England, and when they deviated too much from the central beliefs of Wesleyan theology. More about those central beliefs later. Methodists and other Wesleyans today need to know more about them!

Notes

1. John Wesley, "Preface" to "Sermons on Several Occasions" in *Works,* 1, 105.

2. Ibid., 104.

3. Wesley, "Of Good Angels," *Works,* 3, 8, 13; Wesley, "On the Fall of Man," *Works,* 2, 407.

4. John Wesley, *A Survey of the Wisdom of God in the Creation: A Compendium of Natural Philosophy,* New York: B, Bangs and T. Mason for the Methodist Epis-

copal Church, 1823, 447-448. The several volumes of this work were originally written by others, but Wesley edited them and fully endorsed their contents. In later printings, though not in the first, they were republished in Wesley's own name. So, quotes from them are treated here as direct quotes from Wesley himself.

   5. Ibid., 2, 139.

   6. Wesley, "The Imperfection of Human Knowledge," *Works*, 2, 568.

   7. Wesley, "On Charity," *Works*, 3, 299.

   8. Wesley, "God's Approbation of His Works," *Works*, 2, 387.

   9. John Wesley, "An Address to the Clergy," in Thomas Jackson, ed., *The Works of John Wesley*, London: Wesleyan Conference Office, 1872, 10, 481.

   10. Ibid., 482.

   11. Ibid., 482-483.

   12. Ibid., 483-486.

   13. Ibid., 486-487.

Chapter 2

Don't Take It All Literally

Wesley expected both ministers and ordinary Christians to "search the scriptures," but he did not expect them to take everything literally. Biblical literalism was definitely not John Wesley's way. Except for fundamentalism, created in the late 19th and early 20th Centuries, most Christian thinkers through the ages, including Wesley, identified many different kinds of language in the Bible. Some scriptures were intended to be taken literally, but, as he acknowledged, much scriptural language is obviously poetic, metaphorical, figurative, or analogical—anything but literal. Today, many Christians, maybe even some Wesleyans, claim that everything in the Bible has to be taken literally. At least, that's what they say, though it is never what they really practice. What did Wesley himself think about Biblical literalism?

Wesley lived before modern biblical critical scholarship had made much progress, but he had many insightful things to say about interpreting the Bible that are highly relevant to us today, just as they were to his contemporaries. He distinguished between the "literal" and the "spiritual" meaning of Biblical texts in his "Address to the Clergy." As he recognized, these meanings are not always the same. Getting from the literal to the spiritual usually requires a lot of hard thinking and astute spiritual discernment.[1]

Wesley's sermons, intended for both ordinary Christians and lay ministers, often expressed and illustrated his *"stated rule in interpreting Scripture."* It was, *"never to depart from the plain, literal sense, unless it implies an absurdity."*[2] Variations on and applications of this rule appear in more than a dozen of his writings.[3] As expressed elsewhere it reads, "This is true, if the literal sense of these Scriptures were absurd, and apparently contrary to reason, then we should be obliged not to interpret them according to the letter, but to look out for a looser meaning."[4] In yet another place, he added, "nor contradicts other Scriptures."[5]

If we shouldn't always take the scriptures literally, what should we do? We should look for a "looser" but deeper spiritual meaning if and when taking them literally would be absurd, but how can we tell when the literal meaning is absurd?

To summarize in advance, it would be absurd to take the scriptures literally, Wesley thought, when this would be contrary to experience, both sensory and religious, when it would be contrary to reason or logic, when the words were never meant to be literal in the first place, that is, when they are obviously "figurative," "analogical," or "after the manner of men," when they say something morally unconscionable, and when they contradict the most fundamental love-affirming scriptures. Some of Wesley's own examples, considered next, will explain and illustrate all of this. Some literalistic absurdities may illustrate two or more of these headings. Ideally, all of these criteria work together in harmony and mutually support one another. Let's see how Wesley applied them.

Being Contrary to Experience

Do you believe that the love of money is the root of all evil? Literally of *all* evil? First Timothy 6:10 says so, but, Wesley insisted, money is definitely not *literally* the *sole* root of *all* evil, because "There are a thousand other roots of evil in the world, as sad experience daily shows."[6]

Daily experience, he thought, demonstrates time and again that there are many causes of, motives for, or roots of evil in addition to the love of money. Blaming everything on money is exaggeration and oversimplification, even if the Bible does it. Experience clearly proves otherwise. The love of money is not the whole or even the main story about sin. Taken literally, this biblical sentence is obviously false. "All" is the troublesome word here; it cannot be taken literally. There are many other real roots of, sources of, and basic motives for wrongdoing. Taking the love of money as literally the "sole root" of every human evil greatly oversimplifies its significance and scope. Everyday human experience plainly shows otherwise. Even so, the *love* of money, not money itself, is evil, as Jesus indicated. Money as such, Wesley thought, is a gracious gift of God, essential for gaining all you can, saving all you can, and giving all you can.

Surprisingly, Wesley appealed here only to daily experience, but he could have appealed also to the Bible itself, or to conscience. The scriptures identify numerous other sources of, motives for, or roots of temptation and wrongdoing—for example, selfishness, weakness of will, lust, greed, envy, hatred, lying, idolatry, blasphemy, to name just a few. Human motives for violating most of the Ten Commandments usually have little if anything to do with the love of money. Being contrary to other scriptures is another good reason why "all evil" in this verse cannot be taken literally. Doing so would be contrary to the scriptures.

Being Contrary to Reason

Wesley was not a religious irrationalist. Unlike Martin Luther, neither Calvin nor Wesley rejected the uses of reason in religion or elsewhere. An irrational religion could never be a true religion, Wesley insisted. He would never say—with Tertullian, Luther, and (later) Kierkegaard—that Christians do or should believe things precisely because they are absurd, irrational, or logically self-contradictory. Remember, Wesley was a logician.

Wesley thought a lot about what reason is and how it works—in religion, and everywhere else. Reason, as he understood it, is purely formal. It provides no content of its own. Given his knowledge of and respect for logic, we can paraphrase his account of "reason" in the following way. Reason consists of logical structures, forms, and patterns of thinking, but it has or gives no substantive truths of its own. Being rational involves 1. having ideas or concepts of things, 2. combining them into sentences, or into what Wesley, the logician, often called "propositions" or "premises," 3. then arranging these into evidence-giving or reason-giving patterns of thought—logical arguments, we might say, though Wesley would have said "demonstrations," 4. and then drawing logically correct inferences or conclusions from them, or making "deductions" as Wesley said.[7] Since purely formal reason has or gives no content of its own, *all subject matter* reasoned about must be supplied by other sources such as sensory experience, religious experience, moral experience (conscience), or divine revelations.

For Wesley, being "contrary to reason" meant being poorly or unclearly conceived or understood, or being logically incoherent or self-contradictory, or being concluded in illogical ways, or being inferred from confused, oversimplified, excessively complex, or plainly false premises. Taking some scriptures literally would be contrary to reason whenever any such irrationalities are involved. Scriptures that are contrary to reason when taken literally might also be at odds with experience, conscience, or even more fundamental scriptures.

One obvious instance of scriptures contrary to reason when taken literally is the biblical view of how the starry heavens, the sun, and the earth are arranged in relation to one another. As biblical scholars indicate, in many places, the Bible assumes the reality of a very small and young "three story universe." Throughout the Bible, the flat earth is regarded as the center of the universe; the heavens, sun, moon, and stars, circulate daily around it; and a third layer of water or fire is beneath it.[8] He did not speak of the "three story universe" in just those words, but Wesley did not take any of these scriptures literally.

The earth as the center of the universe is now known as the "Ptolemaic theory." Luther and Calvin still believed in it, but Wesley definitely rejected it. He favored the decidedly non-biblical but more scientific Copernican theory. It denies that our earth is the center of the universe and that the sun, stars, and heavens revolve around it. It says that the sun is the center of our solar system, and our earth revolves around it. Wesley preferred Copernicanism because it is more reasonable, simpler, and more in accord with experience than the biblical cosmology. As he explained,

> The Copernican system is now generally received, which supposes the sun to be fixed in the centre, without any other motion, than that round his own axis. . . . This system is extremely simple and natural, and easily accounts for most phenomena. . . . It is more rational to suppose the earth moves round the sun, than that the huge bodies of the planets and of the sun itself, and the immense firmament of stars, should all move round the inconsiderable body of earth every four and twenty hours.[9]

Being "contrary to reason" was not the same thing for Wesley as being "beyond reason." *All* truths are beyond reason in the sense that reason itself is purely formal and yields no substantive content, knowledge, or truths whatsoever. All legitimate truth claims are derived from experience, or revelation, or conscience (our moral sense)—not from reason alone. Rationalistic philosophers say that all by itself, reason yields definite truths—usually called "intuitions," "innate ideas," or "self-evident truths"—quite apart from all experience. Wesley did not stand within that rationalistic philosophical tradition.[10]

Wesley was a philosophical "empiricist," who grounded all knowledge (except revelation) in experience—sensory, religious, introspective, or moral. Wesley agreed with many Roman Catholic thinkers, for example, St. Thomas Aquinas, that revealed truths are beyond reason, but they are not inherently irrational, that is, they are not logically incoherent or self-contradictory. He disagreed in effect with those like Tertullian, Luther, and (later) Kierkegaard, who said we should believe Christian doctrines precisely because they are inherently absurd, logically incoherent, or otherwise irrational.

Wesley explicitly rejected Martin Luther's claim that "Reason is a whore." In direct defiance of Luther, Wesley affirmed both reason *and* revelation; he said he wanted *both* in religion.[11] Luther allowed for reason in everyday affairs, but not in religion. About religion, Wesley affirmed to the contrary, "It is a fundamental principle with us, that to renounce reason is to renounce religion; that religion and reason go hand in hand, and that all irrational religion is false religion."[12] He argued that we cannot even understand or interpret the Bible, much less solve any of our moral problems, without relying on reason.[13] A great deal of reasoning goes on within the Bible itself, he claimed; both Jesus and Paul were rationally competent thinkers who regularly reasoned with their hearers.[14]

With all its limitations, Wesley's reliance on reason in both religion and elsewhere was perfectly compatible with his emphasis on mystery and human fallibility, that is, on how much we do not know and are never likely to know on our own.

Obviously Non-literal Language

Do you believe you are literally eating the body and drinking the blood of Christ when you take Communion? The Lord's Supper is accompanied by the words, "This is my body" (Matthew 26:26, Mark 14:22, Luke 22:19, I. Corinthians 11:24). Do you take that literally? Roman Catholics are supposed to believe the bread is literally Christ's body. Their communion wafers look, taste, smell, and touch just like ordinary wafers. Nevertheless, they are literally the body of Christ, so their church teaches. They take Jesus' words quite literally, "Take, eat, this is my body." This is one part of the Bible that no Protestants take literally!

Wesley himself definitely did not believe this to be literally true, or that Jesus even meant for it to be understood that way. He emphatically rejected the Roman Catholic doctrine of transubstantiation. He said that Jesus "in figurative language, . . . calls this bread his body" and that the bread is only a "sign" that "signifies or represents" his body, not the real thing.[15] Taking these words literally confuses mere signs with the realities they symbolize. Also, Wesley thought, our senses show us that communion bread is not human flesh, and God gave us reliable senses. Literalism just does not work here. Transubstantiation is *absurd*.

Wesley identified many words in the Bible as non-literal because they are so obviously "figurative" (metaphorical) or "spoken after the manner of men." Figurative expressions say that one thing *is* or is *like* another, without meaning they literally *are* exactly the same thing, or that they have precisely the same powers, qualities, and relations. For example, "birth" literally refers to the physical beginnings of life, but, extended metaphorically, it can symbolize spiritual beginnings. These "births" resemble one other despite obvious differences. Jesus himself, Wesley thought, well understood that he sometimes used figures of speech, not literal language. Jesus quite self-consciously warned Nicodemus not to take him literally when he spoke of being "born again."[16]

Wesley identified many other scriptural words that have only figurative but not literal significance. The book of Revelation at the end of the *New Testament* is riddled with figures of speech, as he indicated. "Figurative(ly)" appears seventeen times in his commentary on that book. Consider just one example. Many words describing the "new Jerusalem" in Revelation 21:15 are very obviously non-literal. According to Wesley, "The gold, the pearls, the precious stones, the walls, foundations, gates, are undoubtedly figurative expressions."[17] Metaphorical biblical language was never intended to be taken literally in the first place.

Consider one more example of figurative words and expressions in the Bible that should not be taken literally. Like virtually all Christian thinkers before him, Wesley insisted that God is a disembodied or incorporeal spirit. This means that God has no spatial qualities or dimensions whatsoever—no physical size, shape, weight, motion, position, etc. God definitely does not have a large-scale humanoid body. God is not literally like a handsome old man sitting on a throne somewhere. When he explained the "image of God" in Genesis 1:27, Wesley emphatically denied that God looks like us physically—because *God has no body at all.* God is a disembodied spirit.

> That man was made in God's image, and after his likeness; two words to express the same thing. God's image upon man, consists, in his nature, not that of his body, for God has not a body, but that of his soul. The soul is a spirit, an intelligent, immortal spirit, an active spirit, herein resembling God, the Father of spirits, and the soul of the world.[18]

If God has no body, it follows that God's showing only his back-side, etc., to Moses in Exodus 33:22-23 is figurative or metaphorical speech, (as are all physical images of and words for God in the Bible and elsewhere). In this story "hand," "face," and "back-side" are expressed only "after the manner of men,"[19] Wesley claimed. These words are culture-bound and potentially misleading metaphors, he thought. Wesley knew that in the Bible God is often said to have human-like body parts—eyes, ears, hands, arms, a right hand side, a back side, and so on. But we should take none of that literally. As he explained, "The words, figuratively transferred from one thing to another, do not agree with the things to which they are transferred, in . . . their literal sense. So hands and eyes, when applied to God, are not spoke in any part of their literal signification."[20] He did not say so, but this also applies to God's literal masculinity or femininity. Wesley did not get into that!

Despite all of his caution, Wesley took some things in the Bible literally that we could not believe to be literally true today. Clear examples are his unquestioning acceptance of the six days of creation in Genesis 1, and that Adam and Eve originally lived in a flawless Eden where there was no sin, death, struggle, conflict, pain, suffering, or immorality of any kind. Today we know that the dinosaurs, other animals, and other life forms lived, struggled, suffered, and died for vast eons of time before human beings ever appeared on earth.

Notes

1. Wesley, "An Address to the Clergy," Jackson, 10, 483, 491, 492, 493.
2. Wesley, "Of the Church," *Works*, 3, 50. Italics added.
3. Ibid., 1, 473, n. 22.
4. Wesley, "The Love of God," *Works*, 4, 337.
5. Wesley, "A Call to Backsliders," *Works*, 3, 215; and Wesley, "Upon our Lord's Sermon on the Mount," *Works*, 1, 473.
6. Wesley, "Upon Our Lord's Sermon on the Mount, I," *Works*, 1, 476.
7. This paraphrases Wesley, "The Case of Reason Impartially Considered," *Works*, 2, 593.
8. For example, see: Genesis 1:8-10, 14-18, Isaiah 40:22, Job 22:14, 26:7-14; 28:24; Proverbs 8:26-29; Mark 16:19, Luke 16:23-24, 26, Acts 1:9-11, and Revelation 4:1-2, 12:7-12, 20:1, 3, 10.
9. Wesley, *A Survey of the Wisdom of God in the Creation: A Compendium of Natural Philosophy*, 2, 110.
10. Wesley, "On the Discoveries of Faith," *Works*, 4, 29.
11. Wesley, "Journal," Nov. 27, 1750.
12. Wesley, "A Letter to the Rev. Dr. Rutherford," March 28, 1768, *Works*, 9, 382.
13. Wesley, "Salvation by Faith," *Works*, 1, 119.
14. Wesley, "An Earnest Appeal to Men of Reason and Religion," *Works*, 11, 56.
15. John Wesley, *Explanatory Notes on the New Testament*, http://wesley.nnu.edu/john-wesley/john-wesleys-notes-on-the-bible/ Wesley's comments on Luke 22:19, I. Cor. 1:24, Matthew 26:26.
16. Ibid., comments on John 3:4.
17. Ibid., comment on Revelation 22:15.
18. Ibid., comments on Genesis 1:27.
19. Ibid., comments on Exodus 33:22-23.
20. Wesley, *A Survey of the Wisdom of God in the Creation: A Compendium of Natural Philosophy*, 2, 437.

Chapter 3

Do Take It All Lovingly

Wesley identified many other scriptures that should not be taken literally. Indeed, some should not be taken at all—those clearly contrary to conscience and love.

Have you ever wondered what conscience is or how it works? Do you ever let your conscience be your guide? Wesley thought a lot about such things, and he can help us to understand them.

Wesley believed firmly in both conscience and love, and he assumed that they work in harmony. As for *conscience*, everyone everywhere is born with one, he thought, and it begins to function fairly early in life. When he considered conscience as universally present, Wesley called it "natural;" but regarded as a special gift from God, it was "supernatural."

Here is how he explained conscience: "It is a kind of silent reasoning of the mind, whereby those things which are judged to be right are approved of with pleasure; but those which are evil are disapproved of with uneasiness," and it is "found in every man born into the world."[1] Conscience belongs to experience, to our moral sense, not to reason. Yet, it is not irrational, just as ordinary sense experience is not irrational. By God's prevenient grace, everyone has it, though not always to the same degree, just as we do have any of our "external" senses to exactly the same degree. Conscience is often undeveloped. It is easily suppressed, and it is often muffled, undermined, or distorted by our sinful desires and dispositions. Social forces and conventions (upbringing and peer pressures) may work against it. We may also deliberately harden our hearts against it. It typically needs to be restored or elevated to its proper level of functioning. Yet, when properly restored, developed, informed, and enlightened, conscience is a precious inner compass given to us by God to guide us in matters of right and wrong, good and evil. It is a still small voice of God within us.

If Wesley was right about how it works, how can we bring the still small voice of conscience to bear upon our own moral lives? It operates when we focus our minds and hearts on some action, situation, or principle, and then ask ourselves, after careful consideration, if we conscientiously approve of it with pleasure or disapprove of it with uneasiness. Let's try this out to see if conscience helps us to interpret and deal properly with some troublesome scriptures, and also helps us to live better Christian lives. Non-Christians can also try it out because degrees of conscience are universally present in all lands and nations by God's prevenient grace. Try listening to your own conscience when dealing with your own moral and scriptural problems.

Morally Unconscionable Scriptures

As Wesley said, "There are some Scriptures which more immediately commend themselves to every man's conscience"[2] than others, so conscience can help us decide when to affirm some scriptures and when to have reservations about others. Let us consider a few biblical examples that Wesley found troublesome to conscience.

Do you believe that women should *not* be allowed to speak in Church? That is what St. Paul taught (I. Corinthians 14:34-35, I. Timothy 2:11-12). Do you approve or disapprove of this in your own mind, heart, and conscience after very careful consideration? In accord with these scriptures, but perhaps not with conscience, some churches today rule out women preachers. Female Sunday school teachers (who also literally speak in church) seem to be OK, but not female preachers. John Wesley struggled with the issue of women preachers. He originally opposed allowing women to preach, as did most ministers of his day. After wrestling conscientiously for a long time with this issue, he finally allowed talented women evangelists to preach in his Methodist Societies. He also admitted at least two to be regular ministers in the "Methodist Connexion." This was a radical step forward for his time and place. Relying on his personal experience with gifted women preachers, as well as on his own conscience, Wesley concluded that St. Paul's discrimination against women preachers was morally unconscionable.

Now consider another serious case. Do you believe that wives should be subordinated to their husbands in literally *all* things? St. Paul affirmed such total dominance of men over women in Ephesians 5:22-24. (Compare Genesis 3:16.)

What does your conscience say about this? Wesley clearly disagreed with St. Paul about it on grounds of conscience. Conscience, he insisted, has a vital and authoritative role to play in limiting the subordination of wives to husbands, or what he called "the duty of wives to obey their husbands." In Wesley's view, St. Paul had not really thought this through far enough. What would St. Paul say, Wesley asked, if a husband demanded that his wife cease being a Christian, that she "renounce *her way* of worshipping God"? In Wesley's words, "What would St Paul have said to a wife whose husband forbade her to "follow 'this way' any more?" Wesley's response was, "Our own conscience gives you the answer." Our own conscience clearly prohibits such absolute obedience and submissiveness, no matter what the Bible says about it. Wesley claimed that even St. Paul's conscience would have given the same answer if he had really thought it through. So, indeed, would the conscience of "our Savior"![3]

Does your own conscience tell you that a wife should obey her husband even if he demands that she do something flagrantly immoral or unchristian, something forbidden by her own conscience, something like worshipping false gods, or selling herself into prostitution? Should she obey? The still small voice of any enlightened conscience should tell us that such absolute obedience, such complete subordination of wives to husbands, is just plain wrong, no matter what St. Paul said about it. Wouldn't your own conscience disapprove of this? Wesley's did.

With wives, families, and conscience in mind, Wesley affirmed that "Reason and persuasion are the only weapons you ought to use, even toward your own wife and children."[4] Yes, the *only* weapons. If so, then in no circumstances could husbands ever use their sheer power and authority as husbands to compel their wives to obey or to do anything. Reason and persuasion are their *only* legitimate "weapons." Both conscience and love forbid men to use any other kind of power over women, indeed, over anyone. Coercion is always unconscionable. The total submission of wives to husbands in literally *"all things"* cannot be derived from and is not compatible with "Love your neighbor as yourself," (Matthew 22:39, Mark 12:31, Luke 10:27), or "as I have loved you," as Jesus once said, (John 13:34), or from "Do unto others as you would have them do unto you" (Matthew 7:12, Luke 6:31). Applying this Golden Rule involves imagining yourself to have their beliefs, thoughts, feelings, projects, responsibilities, and commitments; it does not work if you just imagine them has having yours. In applying the Golden Rule, Wesley said, you must suppose "yourself to be just as he is now."[5] Or "she," we must add. For Wesley, these were the most fundamental principles of Christian ethics, and he often appealed to them.[6] Conscience itself affirms and accords with these scriptural principles and uses them to interpret and assess other scriptures.

In one discussion, Wesley strongly objected to "using" women, that is, to treating them as mere things, mere playthings, (sex toys?), mere means to ulterior ends not their own, mere objects—while not respecting and honoring them as subjects. St. Paul can also be quoted on this opposite (and more conscionable) side of the moral status of women (Galatians 3:28), as Wesley does below.

> Herein there is no difference: 'there is neither male nor female in Christ Jesus'. Indeed, it has long passed for a maxim with many that 'women are only to be seen, not heard.' And accordingly many of them are brought up in such a manner as if they were only designed for agreeable playthings! But is this doing honour to the sex? Or is it a real kindness to them? No; it is the deepest unkindness; it is horrid cruelty; it is mere Turkish barbarity. And I know not how any woman of sense and spirit can submit to it. Let all you that have it in your power assert the right which the God of nature has given you. Yield not to that vile bondage any longer. You, as well as men, are rational creatures. You, like them, were made in the image of God: you are equally candidates for immortality. You too are called of God, as you have time, to 'do good unto all men'.[7]

Wesley did not always live up to the very best of his own moral and spiritual insights. He realized this himself! Unlike his brother, Charles, he did not have a good marriage or any children—for many reasons. His wife was beyond child-bearing age by the time they were married in 1751. Their relations were so strained that she left him periodically, beginning in 1771. She said she was never coming back, though she did. Finally, she left him for good. One reason for their disharmony was that she suspected him of emotional if not physical infidelity. Her suspicions were not unjustified. Another reason was that he pulled a St. Paul-at-his-worst on her! He was a very domineering husband. In a letter to her, written on March 23, 1760, he claimed that he had a husband's right to her absolute obedience. He informed her, "[E]very act of disobedience is an act of rebellion against God and the King, as well as against Your affectionate Husband."[8] If you haven't figured it out yet, telling your wife that disobedience to you is equivalent to disobedience to God is not a very effective way to win her heart! No wonder she finally left him! Sadly, Wesley did not always practice what he preached, but this does not mean that what he preached about the equality of women was wrong.

Wesley's rejection of some scriptures on grounds of conscience is highly relevant to many Biblical and moral issues that Wesley himself did not directly address. Indeed, it is highly relevant today. Those who know what is actually there in the Bible fully understand this. Consider one of the most serious problems confronting the Methodist Church in the 21st Century, one that threatens to divide us again—the LGBTQ issue. Wesley knew only about the "G" part of this, at best. His one letter symbol for it would have been "S" for "sodomy." Consider this representative quote from one of his sermons: "It is a small proof of his [the devil's] power that common swearers, drunkards, whoremongers, adulterers, thieves, robbers, sodomites, murderers, are still found in every part of our land."[9] Wesley believed that homosexuality is absolutely wrong on Biblical grounds (Leviticus 18:22; I. Corinthians 6:9-10), as do many people today. He also regarded such dispositions and deeds as purely voluntary yet wrongful choices like swearing, drinking, robbing, and the other vices in his list. His understanding of it never went any deeper than that.

Today, we know much more about homosexuality than St. Paul and Wesley did. Most of us know from our own experience that our heterosexual dispositions are not voluntary choices. We are just born with them. We also understand today that homosexual dispositions are not voluntary either, but Wesley did not know that. He always listed it along with other *voluntary* sins. So did St. Paul. In reality, our sexual orientations are given to us by our genes, brain, physiology, and God. Some of us have one of these gifts for loving, some the other, some in between. Our actions based on these dispositions may be voluntary and under our control, but not the dispositions themselves. Both heterosexuality and homosexuality can be expressed and lived faithfully and lovingly. Both can also be greatly abused. In numbers alone, there is far more heterosexual abuse in the world than homosexual. If we are worried that homosexuals will abuse and corrupt our children or other loved ones, we should be much more concerned that heterosexuals will do it.

But isn't the Bible against it? Yes, but the Bible was mistaken in affirming total male dominance over women. It was also wrong in allowing slavery, as long as masters are good to their slaves, and slaves are obedient to their masters (Ephesians 6:5-9). This was good enough for Methodists in the South (and some in the North) before the Civil War. Of course, they often ignored the "be good to your slaves" part. Also, enslaving anyone in the first place always falls far short of being good to them, but neither St. Paul nor Southern slave owners acknowledged that. In the mid-1840s, the Methodist Church divided into South and North over this very issue. Both sides read the same Bible and prayed to the same God, which Abraham Lincoln later said of our divided nation during the Civil War era.

Conscience tells *us* that slavery is wrong (as is racism). It probably told earlier slave owners the same thing, but most ignored conscience for worldly gains. Wesley conscientiously opposed both slavery[10] and the complete subordination of wives to their husbands in all things. Slavery was commonplace and never condemned in the Old and New Testaments, not even by Jesus. In much of the Bible women were regarded and treated as property, not as persons. Exodus 21:7-8 allows fathers to sell their daughters into slavery, and to redeem them later if they are not pleasing to their buyers and masters. Are you ready to be completely faithful to the Bible about that? Jesus never dealt with the slavery issue directly, so far as we know. Paul allowed it, along with the absolute dominance of husbands over wives. In good conscience, Wesley did not agree. Did Jesus not come to set us free from unloving and unconscionable laws and scriptures?

Most Christians today who oppose homosexuality on biblical grounds are really not willing to go all the way with what the Bible says about it. The Bible condemns homosexuality in both Testaments; *it also says very clearly that all homosexuals should be put to death* (Leviticus 20:13). What does your conscience tell you about that? If the Bible is absolutely infallible in condemning homosexuality, why isn't it also absolutely infallible in requiring that all homosexuals be put to death?

Is executing homosexuals really the best way to love our neighbors as ourselves, or to apply the Golden Rule to them? What if we had been born with their desires and dispositions? Does your own conscience approve of putting them to death on Biblical grounds? If it does, then you must also approve of putting to death all who curse or strike their fathers or mothers (Exodus 21: 15, 17), all who sacrifice to false gods (Exodus 22:20), and all who commit adultery—both the men and the women involved (Leviticus 20:10). Would you and all the people you know and care about survive such a biblically-based Holocaust, grounded in an unreflective literal faithfulness to "infallible" scriptures? What does your conscience say about such mass executions? Can either executing homosexuals or regarding homosexuality as always wrong be reconciled with "Love your neighbor as yourself" and "Do unto others as you would have them do unto you?" After all, these are scriptures, too.

Shouldn't we Wesleyans, we Christians, *always* ask, "What is the most loving thing that we as Christians could do?" Isn't the most loving way the most scriptural way, the most rock-bottom Christian way? Would our Methodist church divide over LGBTQ issues if we carefully follow that? Wesley thought that love is the ultimate lens through which Christians should view all moral and spiritual issues. If so, the ultimate Wesleyan-in-spirit question for us about LGBTQ issues is, "What is the most loving way for us today to deal with such people, especially given what we know that Wesley did not know?"

Perhaps the most loving thing that today's Wesleyan conservatives could do would be to ask themselves if they could lovingly and in good conscience execute all homosexuals and all adulterers. Perhaps the most loving thing that Wesleyan progressives could do is to stay within the church and continue to work more patiently and vigorously to make it better and more loving—just as they have been doing. As for those in between, please just stay put in the spirit of "If your heart is as my heart, give me your hand."[11] Here is what Wesley would say to us today: "Though we can't think alike, may we not love alike? May we not be of one heart, though we are not of one opinion? Without all doubt we may."[12]

In addition to being morally unconscionable, sexism, slavery, racism, and all unjust discrimination cannot be reconciled with key verses of scripture like "Love your neighbor as yourself" and "Do unto others as you would have them do unto you."

Unloving Scriptures that Conflict with Loving Scriptures

If we can't take everything in the Bible literally, how then should we take it? Wesley's answer was, *We should always take everything lovingly.* Even metaphorical language should be interpreted lovingly, where possible. His most fundamental principle of biblical interpretation was, *"No Scripture can mean that God is not love, or that his mercy is not over all his works."*[13] But what does this mean doctrinally and in practice? How did Wesley apply it? How should we?

Wesley did not say this, but inspirations may be only the beginning points of inquiry, not the infallible end points of our quest for religious or other kinds of knowledge. Wesley himself said, "All Scripture is given by inspiration of God," and occasionally he affirmed that the scriptures are "unquestionably true."[14] However, in practice and in many writings, he clearly did not equate inspiration with infallibility or literalism. Some scriptures are just plain absurd when taken literally, he recognized. In such cases, we must "look for a looser meaning." But does it stop there? Should some scriptures be outright rejected as unloving? Can every troublesome text always be given a "looser" loving meaning that reconciles it with more fundamental scriptural truths? Maybe some scriptures should just be rejected "flat out" because they contradict the most basic of all biblical, moral, and spiritual insights and truths. Wesley did not say this explicitly, but in practice he actually did dismiss some unloving scriptures outright. Some scriptures just cannot be given any Christian meaning at all, not even a looser one, that will harmonize them with love, reason, experience, conscience, and carefully selected traditions. What are some of these?

Wesley said that "scripture interprets scripture."[15] In practice, he also allowed reason, experience, and conscience to interpret scripture. He regarded some scriptures as more basic than others. All accounts of "progressive revelation" assume as much. In the "Sermon on the Mount" (Matthew 5-7), Jesus himself definitely rejected some Old Testament scriptures. Even Jesus said we can't believe everything in the Bible (like "an eye for an eye") as "was said by them of old"! Some scriptural texts are absurd when taken literally, Wesley recognized. Some are less clear than others. Some are logically incompatible with conscience, the love commandments, and other truly fundamental Christian convictions. Other scriptures, of course, do actually express and affirm genuine basics. Christian wisdom lies in knowing how to recognize them. The scriptures do not always speak with one voice. We can't cover everything here, but we can identify the most fundamental of all fundamentals as Wesley understood them.

The most essential truth about God in the Bible, Wesley thought, is that "God is love" (I John 4:7, 16). Wesley regarded love as God's "reigning attribute, the attribute that sheds an amiable glory on all His other perfections."[16] The most fundamental normative truths in the Bible are the two love commandments of Jesus. Everything in the Bible, Wesley thought, should be judged "in proportion to the nearness of its relation to what is there laid down as the sum of all—the love of God and our neighbors."[17] Many times Wesley identified the two love commandments as rock-bottom Christianity, Methodism, and "true religion."[18]

We must now consider two more scriptures that Wesley rejected altogether because logically they cannot be reconciled with God's love. Not even God himself could obey the two love commandments, yet stand behind these troublesome scriptures, Wesley thought.

First, as Wesley recognized, St. Paul taught that *the elect*, the chosen few, are predestined for Heaven, and the rest of humankind are doomed to Hell. Read the eighth and ninth chapters of Paul's book of Romans. We will return to predestination later, but it affirms basically that from all eternity God arbitrarily destined most people for Hell and only a chosen few for Heaven. *Wesley himself did not believe that a loving God could do that.*

Closely related was another troublesome-to-Wesley scriptural affirmation. Malachi 1:2-3 and Romans 9:13. Both say that God loved Jacob but hated Esau. Wesley out-and-out rejected both predestination and God's hatred of Esau because they are insufferably unloving. Yes, they are in the Bible, but they are logically incompatible with "God is love," the most fundamental of all theological truths. As he explained below, sometimes the Bible contradicts itself. As a logician, Wesley knew a contradiction when he saw one!

> And as this doctrine [predestination] manifestly and directly tends to overthrow the whole Christian revelation, so it does the same thing, by plain consequence, in making that revelation contradict itself. For it is grounded on such an interpretation of some texts (more or fewer it matters not) as flatly contradict all the other texts, and indeed the whole scope and tenor of Scripture. For instance: the asserters of this doctrine interpret that text of Scripture, 'Jacob have I loved, but Esau I have hated," as implying that God in a literal sense hated Esau and all the reprobated from eternity. Now what can possibly be a more flat contradiction than this, not only to the whole scope and tenor of Scripture, but also to all those particular texts which expressly declare, 'God is love'?[19]

In effect, Wesley thought, no Biblical text is true, literally or otherwise, if it is incompatible with logic, experience, and conscience, or with God's love, justice, mercy, and goodness. Such biblical "truths" would be ultimate absurdities! Can you think of any other troublesome things in the Bible that should be reconsidered in the light of love?

Notes

1. Wesley, "On Conscience," *Works*, 3, 481.
2. Wesley, "On Charity," *Works*, 3, 292.
3. Wesley, "A Farther Appeal to Men of Reason and Religion, Part I," *Works*, 11, 189.
4. Ibid., 190.
5. Wesley, "Upon Our Lord's Sermon on the Mount, X," *Works*, 1, 661.
6. In the first volume alone of Wesley's *Works*, the second love commandment is invoked on pages 137, 211, 221, 387, 401, 427, 509, and perhaps elsewhere. The Golden Rule is invoked on pages 133, 171, 173, 273, 341, 372, 499, 565, 587, 650, 669, and perhaps elsewhere.
7. Wesley, "On Visiting the Sick," *Works*, 3, 396.
8. John Telford, ed., *The Letters of John Wesley*, London: Epworth Press, 1931, 4, March 23, 1760.

9. Wesley, "A Caution against Bigotry," *Works,* 2, 67–68.

10. John Wesley, *Thoughts Upon Slavery*, London: Joseph Crookshank, 1773. Four days before his death, Wesley wrote his very last letter to William Wilberforce, a Member of Parliament, encouraging him to oppose England's participation in the slave trade.

11. 2 Kings 10:15 was Wesley's text for his great sermon on universal or catholic Christianity, "Catholic Spirit," *Works*, 2, 81.

12. Wesley, "Catholic Spirit," *Works,* 2, 82.

13. Wesley, "Free Grace," *Works*, 3, 556.

14. Wesley, "On Corrupting the Word of God," *Works*, 4, 249; "On Charity," *Works* 3, 292.

15. Wesley, "An Address to the Clergy," Jackson, 10, 482; Wesley, *Works*, 2, 501.

16. Wesley, *Explanatory Notes on the New Testament,* Wesley's comment on 1 John 4:8.

17. Wesley, "On Laying the Foundations of the New Chapel," *Works*, 3, 587-588.

18. Wesley, "A Plain Account of Genuine Christianity," in Albert C. Outler, ed., *John Wesley*, New York: Oxford University Press, 1964, 184-185; Wesley, "The Character of a Methodist," *Works*, 9, 35, 37-38; Wesley, "The Way to the Kingdom," *Works*, 1, 221-224.

19. Wesley, "Free Grace," *Works*, 3, 552.

CHAPTER 4

POOR FAITH: BELIEFS WITHOUT WORKS AND LOVE

Christians are often called "believers," but what are believers? And why are Christians not called "lovers," "doers," or "servers" instead of just "believers"? Wesley did recognize that Christians are believers. He also understood that "believing" or "having faith" can mean many different things. He considered at least two such meanings, and he thought one to be far preferable to the other. The first is that faith consists solely in mentally affirming or believing Christian doctrines to be true. The other is "the faith that works by love," words used by St. Paul (Galatians 5:6) and cited many times by Wesley. Let's call them "poor faith" and "good faith," though these were not Wesley's own words. This chapter is about poor faith, beliefs without works and love

Poor Faith as Mental Assent to the Doctrines of Christian Orthodoxy

As Wesley knew, many Christians, both Catholic and Protestant, think that having faith is a matter of believing or mentally assenting to the truth of the doctrines of Christian orthodoxy, or to Christian "fundamentals." This kind of faith is purely mental or systemic. It is merely a matter of affirming certain doctrines to be true "with the top of one's head," so to speak. The Catholic version of it says that faith is the assent of the intellect to the truth of the doctrines taught by the church. "Back to the Bible" Protestants say that faith is mental acceptance of or assent to the doctrines of the Bible—every last one of them taken literally, if you are a fundamentalist. But not every Christian is a fundamentalist.

Wesley often identified and discussed what he understood to be the most basic Christian doctrines derived from revelation or the scriptures. The contents of his lists vary. In one sermon the "capital doctrines," of Christian orthodoxy were said to be "the fall of man, justification by faith, . . . the atonement made by the death of Christ, and of his righteousness transferred to them."[1] Other fundamental beliefs were identified in other writings. We are familiar already with his "rock bottom" list of love scriptures.

At times Wesley called all Christian doctrines "opinions," even those most basic. He defined *"orthodoxy"* itself as *"right opinions."*[2] At other times, he distinguished between core Christian beliefs and less essential beliefs. Then, only the less essential beliefs were called "opinions." Either way, "opinions" were the mental, doctrinal, or conceptual parts of Christianity (and of everything else) as far as Wesley was concerned. Viewed philosophically, ideas, beliefs, doctrines, rules, truths, formalities, systems, and conceptual knowledge are "systemic values." Wesley's purpose was not to contrast the certainty of "knowledge" with less certain "opinions." He meant only that all opinions, beliefs, ideas, and doctrines are thoughts in our minds. Christian doctrines are purely conceptual or systemic Christian values. Their realities and functions are purely mental and symbolic. They point us toward realities beyond themselves. They guide us abstractly and symbolically toward authentic living and loving in the real presence of God and our neighbors.

Faith in this minimal sense is mental assent to the truth of "opinions," some essential, some not, some more certain, some less. This is "poor faith" because conceptual or mental believing does not matter nearly as much as actually living, loving, and doing good in loving ways. What really matters is the "faith that works by love," Wesley thought. Mere assent to the truth of revealed doctrines is not a "saving faith," he believed. Believing matters, but it is not the most important aspect of true religion, real Christian faith, and authentic Methodism. True religion is primarily a matter of the heart, not of the head. Both are indispensable, but the head serves the heart.

Ephesians 2:8 says, "For by grace are ye saved through faith; and that not of yourselves: it is the gift of God." Does "faith" here mean nothing more than assenting to the truth of Christian doctrines or "opinions"? Protestantism begins with faith, not works, but what does Christian "faith" really mean? According to Wesley,

> Whatsoever the generality of people may think, it is certain that opinion is not religion: no, not right opinion; assent to one or to ten thousand truths. There is a wide difference between them: even right opinion is as distant from religion as the east is from the west. Persons may be quite right in their opinions, yet have no religion at all. And on the other hand persons may be truly religious who hold many wrong opinions but many of them are now real Christians, loving God and all mankind.[3]

Don't you know some very good, kind, honest, just, faithful, and loving Christians who cannot recite, explain, or properly assent mentally to the revealed doctrines of Christian orthodoxy? Don't you also know some rigidly dogmatic people at the other extreme? They can explain and adamantly assert whole pages and chapters of systematic theology—but they are still really nasty, selfish, hateful, unfair, prejudiced, unsympathetic, untrustworthy, and unloving people. If so, then you understand what Wesley was getting at!

Wesley had one decisive argument, he thought, against equating real Christian faith with affirming orthodox Christian doctrines to be true. As suggested by James 2:19, *the devils resolutely believe in God and assent to the truth of absolutely everything in the Bible and in the Creeds!*[4] If you want to find a true believer, go to the Devil! Intellectually, the devils absolutely affirm and believe all revealed Christian truths. Surely real faith, saving faith, is something more than this! Faith, properly understood, Wesley insisted, "is not (as some have fondly conceived) a bare assent to the truth of the Bible, of the articles of our Creed, or of all that is contained in the Old and New Testament. The devils believe this, as well as I or thou; and yet they are devils still."[5] A person can be "as orthodox as the devil,"[6] he said, and still not be a good Christian!

What do real Christians have that the devils do not have? It is the "faith that works by love." The devils totally assent mentally to all Christian beliefs, but inwardly they are very unloving, and outwardly they do very bad things, not good things. Hatred, not love, is their obsession and passion. They do not love God; they do not love every creature God has made; they do not repent of their sins; they do not claim God's grace, redemption, reconciliation, restoration, and forgiveness for themselves.

They do not do good works lovingly. Speaking metaphorically, they do not have Christian hearts. They do have Christian heads.

Real Christianity is primarily a religion of the heart, not of the head, Wesley thought. He advocated Christianity "not as it implies a set of opinions, a system of doctrines, but as it refers to men's hearts and lives."[7] "False religion," he said, "is any religion which does not imply the giving the heart to God. Such is, first, a religion of opinions, or what is commonly called orthodoxy."[8]

Wesley warned more than once that Christians should get their priorities straight. They should learn to rank, evaluate, and even love the various "parts" or "branches" of Christianity in proportion to their real and proper worth.[9] At the very end of the "13th of Corinthians," as Wesley called it, St. Paul himself ranked faith, hope, and love and proclaimed, "The greatest of these is love." Wesley himself often ranked the proper worth of faith (as doctrinal belief), good works, and love. Faith, doctrinally understood, is "only the handmaiden of love. As glorious and honorable as it is, it is not the end of the commandment. God hath given this honor to love alone: love is the end of all of the commandments of God."[10] All genuine Christian doctrines, commandments, and practices express, support, and are given as means to living in love. Wesley wrote, "I regard even faith itself not as an end but a means only. The end of the commandment is love, of every command, of the whole Christian dispensation. Let this love be attained, by whatever means, and I am content; I desire no more. All is well, if we love the Lord our God with all our heart and our neighbor as ourselves."[11]

Wesley compared doctrinal faith with love and ranked it much lower. He wrote of "the superior glory of love, above that of faith." He said, "It [doctrinal faith] loses all its excellence when brought into a comparison with love,"[12] and "For how far is love, even with many wrong opinions, to be preferred before truth itself without love."[13] Obviously, real faith cannot be separated from love; only doctrinal faith can be so separated. Doing so always creates moral and spiritual danger zones.

Doctrinal Faith Alone

Real Christian faith cannot be disconnected from Christian works and Christian love, but a purely doctrinal faith can. Wesley knew some Christians who actually tried to separate them, and he did not like what he saw.

Most Methodists know that John Wesley had some connections with the Moravians. Some of them came from Germany, settled in England, and flourished in London. Others made their way across the Atlantic to the Colonies, often traveling through England on their way. Most of us recall that on his two and a half month or so long journey across the Atlantic to Georgia, Wesley's ship was often beset by storms. Everyone else on board was terrified, but the Moravians remained calm, prayed, and sang hymns. Wesley was most favorably impressed by them then, as he was later when Moravian Peter Böhler advised him to "Preach faith till you have it." But what is "faith"?

After the Great Awakening was well under way, Wesley's earliest Methodist Society in London was combined with and met regularly with the Moravians in a building on Fetter Lane, but that did not last. In 1739, he separated from them, mainly because of their extreme interpretation of salvation by faith alone, *sola fide*, the Lutheran way, and their firm opinion that Christianity requires nothing more of anyone than that. Not all Moravians or Lutherans were this extreme. Nor was Luther himself, but members of one Moravian faction in London led by Philip Molther were. Given the dominance of these Moravians in the combined "Fetter Lane Society," Wesley found it necessary to move his Methodists to a new meeting place, an old and large Foundry, slowly thereafter restructured. It became the Methodist headquarters, meetinghouse, schoolhouse, book room, offices, stables, and free medical clinic in London. It also served for many years as Wesley's permanent residence until new headquarters were built in 1777 and the Foundry was demolished.

Faith alone is enough, these particular Moravians thought. By faith alone are we saved and made acceptable to God. From this, they concluded that they didn't have to *know*, learn, read, or study anything—not the Bible or anything else. They also did not have to *do* anything, not even obey the Ten Commandments. In their opinion, that would be "works righteousness," not salvation by faith through grace. They repudiated "good works," "the law," "the ordinances," and every trace of "works righteousness." They would not attend church services or partake of the sacraments of the Lord's Supper and Baptism. They did not observe or take part any of the "ordinances" or worship practices of the church. Perfect faith *alone* makes anyone a good Christian, they insisted. Before perfect faith arrives, all moral and devotional works are actually sinful; after it arrives, they are unnecessary. For its arrival, one can only wait quietly and patiently. They called this "stillness." They were know-nothing, do-nothing Christians. In technical theological language, they were "quietists" and "antinomians."[14] Quietists do nothing; antinomians think they are not bound by any laws, not even those of the Bible. They were lawless Christians, if that makes any sense at all. Eventually, Wesley reluctantly recognized that these particular Moravians were not what God expected Christians to be. His definitive judgment was, "Beware of 'Moravianism'—the most refined antinomianism that ever was under the sun, and such as I think could only have sprung from the abuse of true Christian experience."[15]

Other Christians in addition to these Moravians downplayed the "works" part of "the faith that works by love." After much reading, reflection, and self-examination, Wesley became highly critical of that part of Christian mysticism that almost exclusively emphasized inwardly experiencing mystical union with God—to the neglect of Christian social ethics and action. To Moravians, mystics, and inactivists of every kind, Wesley would say, "that Christianity is essentially a social religion, and that to turn it into a solitary one is to destroy it," and "to conceal this religion is impossible, as well as utterly contrary to the design of its author."[16]

Yes, with Lutheranism, Wesley did affirm salvation or justification (pardon) by faith, but he had a much richer understanding of the nature of "faith" than many people have. His mature judgment was that the poor faith of belief alone is not enough. A better faith, a truly good faith is required. Saving faith works through love, is informed by proper beliefs, and is nurtured by conscience and moral and devotional practices. Compared to and isolated from "the labours of love" and from love itself, doctrinal faith has little value, though it is still significant within the faith that works by love. Wesley wrote of "the superior glory of love, above that of faith," and "It [cognitive faith] loses all its excellence when brought into a comparison with love."[17]

Now Wesley did not throw out all orthodox beliefs. Carefully selected beliefs are very important, even downright indispensable. Some desirable things are very good while others are much better. Rock-bottom Christianity involves *beliefs*, for example, "God is love," and the two love commandments, Wesley insisted. Yet, these beliefs point to something different from and more valuable than beliefs themselves, toward something more important than the Bible in which these beliefs are recorded. These beliefs call for more than doctrinal assent to the truths of the Bible or of the Church. They point toward the *realities* of God, Christ, human beings, and all of God's creatures; and they enable us to live in personal relationships with these realities. As Wesley realized, these realities and our intense, constant, personal, loving, just, compassionate, and lived involvements with them are of much greater value to God himself, to us, and in themselves, than our mere *beliefs* about them, our mental symbols for them.

Christian beliefs, words, and ideas are indispensable symbols or signposts pointing us toward spiritual realities beyond themselves. They really do have an important job to do. They mediate mentally between us and those realities, and they guide us toward them. The love commandments do not tell us to love the love commandments, or the Book in which they are written. They tell us to love God and our neighbors. The Bible is not just about the Bible. It is about the realities of God, Christ, ourselves, and much else. Faith should center on its "proper objects," Wesley said, and "Christ, and God through Christ, are the proper objects of it."[18] True faith is in these realities, not in the symbolical and often metaphorical words and beliefs that mediate between us and them.

Proper Christian faith centers on religious realities, not on "revealed doctrines," "orthodox opinions," or "what the Bible says." It involves much more than mental assent. It is "not a barely speculative, rational thing, a cold, lifeless assent, a train of ideas in the head; but also a disposition of the heart."[19] It further includes a warm *heartfelt love,* as well as dispositional *trust* and *confidence* in God. "The true, living, Christian faith...is not only an assent, an act of the understanding, but a disposition, which God hath wrought in his heart; 'a sure trust and confidence in God that through the merits of Christ his sins are forgiven, and he reconciled to the favor of God';" and faith itself is "'not only a belief of all the articles of our faith, but also a true confidence of the mercy of God, through our Lord Jesus Christ'."[20]

Wesley thought that Christians should not have a warm heart without a cool head, or a cold head without a warm heart. But the head is there to serve the heart.

Notes

1. Wesley, "On Living without God," *Works*, 4, 175.
2. Wesley, "The Way to the Kingdom," *Works*, 1, 220.
3. Wesley, "On the Trinity," *Works*, 2, 374.
4. Wesley, "Salvation by Faith," *Works*, 1, 119-120; Wesley, "The Way to the Kingdom," *Works*, 1, 220, 230; Wesley, "The Marks of the New Birth," *Works*, 1, 418; Wesley, "The Almost Christian," *Works*, 1, 138-139; Wesley, "On Faith," *Works*, 3, 497; Wesley, "On the Wedding Garment," *Works*, 4, 146.
5. Wesley, "The Way to the Kingdom," *Works*, 1, 230; Wesley, "The Marks of the New Birth," *Works*, 1, 418-419.
6. Wesley, "The Way to the Kingdom," *Works*, 1, 220.
7. Wesley, "Scriptural Christianity," *Works*, 1, 161.
8. Wesley, "The Unity of the Divine Being," *Works*, 4, 66.
9. Wesley, "On Zeal," *Works*, 3, 312-315.
10. Wesley, "The Law Established Through Faith," *Works*, 2, 38.
11. Wesley, "To John Smith, June 25, 1746," section 9, *Works*, 26.
12. Wesley, "The Law Established Through Faith," *Works*, 2, 29.
13. Wesley, "Preface," in *Works*, 1, 107.
14. Rem B. Edwards, *John Wesley's Values—And Ours*, Lexington, KY: Emeth Press, 2012. See the selection from Wesley's "Journals" in Outler, 356-357.
15. Outler, 302.
16. Wesley, "Upon Our Lord's Sermon on the Mount, IV," *Works*, 1, 533.
17. Wesley, "The Law Established Through Faith," *Works*, 2, 39.
18. Wesley, "Salvation by Faith," *Works*, 1, 120.
19. Ibid., *Works*, 2, 39.
20. Wesley, "The Marks of the New Birth," *Works*, 1, 418-419.

CHAPTER 5

GOOD FAITH THAT WORKS BY LOVE

Good faith, saving faith, does not separate believing from doing and loving. It unites them so closely that no one of them even makes good sense in complete isolation from the others. Good faith is the "faith that works through love" (Galatians 5:6).

The Faith that Works

Properly understood, saving Christian "faith" includes more than inward believing alone, despite what some of the Moravians thought. Real faith is inseparable from good works, from the faith that works. Wesley insisted that "cold, lifeless assent, a train of ideas in the head," doesn't even count as faith when divorced from good works. As James 2:20 said, "Faith without works is dead." In that light, Wesley wrote, "We esteem no faith but that 'which worketh by love.'"[1] Not "esteeming" something to be faith means not even judging or recognizing it to be faith. Such so-called "faith" does not fulfill the very definition or meaning of "faith," properly understood. It doesn't count as "real faith." Real faith and good works are logically and psychologically intertwined and inseparable. Wesley declared, "For inasmuch as faith without works is dead, it is not faith."[2]

This intimate connection is easy to understand. If you aren't willing to act on something, this means you don't really believe it. You are only paying "lip service" when faith is nothing more than assent to "a train of ideas in the head." Real faith practices what it preaches. As Wesley put it, "See that your practice be in all things suitable to your professions."³ This is why those "do nothing" Moravians repudiated by Wesley were wrong. (Remember, not all Moravians were this extreme.) Real Christian faith involves mental assent, good works, and inner love, all three, but not assent alone. Christian living involves much more than doctrinal assent. Real faith is of much more value to God and to us than believing alone.

Christian ethics deals primarily with good works, and with the principles, motives, and dispositions involved in doing them. The "interior" ideals and motives of Christian ethics consist of commandments, directives, love, compassion, and "all *holy tempers*: long-suffering, gentleness, meekness, goodness, fidelity, temperance—and if any other is comprised in 'the mind which was in Christ Jesus.'"⁴ For Wesley, loving our neighbors as ourselves, doing unto others as we would have them do unto us, developing and practicing the Christian virtues, and imitating Christ and God, were the most basic principles, norms, or guiding ideals of Christian ethics. As for the imitation of Christ, Wesley would have us do as Jesus would do, think as Jesus would think (have the *cognitive* mind of Christ), and love as Jesus would love. All of these were essential to the *complete* mind of Christ.

Good works are the "exterior" parts of Christian ethics. Wesley recognized two kinds of Christian works. First are the moral *Works of Mercy*—acting on the ethical principles just stated for the benefit of "the souls and bodies of men." "By these we exercise all holy tempers." Second are the *Works of Piety*—devotional practices, often called "ordinances." These include "reading and hearing the Word, public, family, private prayer, receiving the Lord's Supper, fasting or abstinence." All Christian works, moral and devotional, are greatly encouraged, socially supported, and carried out through participation in the life of the Church.⁵ Both kinds are genuine means of grace to us and beneficial in many ways to others. By participating in all of them, Christians can both express and grow in the knowledge and love of God and of every creature God has made and loves.

The Faith that Works Through Love

According to Wesley, "In a Christian believer, *love* sits upon the throne, which is erected in the inmost soul; namely, love of God and man, which fills the whole heart and reigns without a rival."[6] Love is the ultimate inner Christian motive or disposition for both religious devotion and moral goodness. God sets high standards of perfection. *Christian perfection* has always been an important theme in Wesleyan theology, but what is it? Do we ever achieve it? Wesley took Jesus very seriously when he said we should be perfect as our Father in Heaven is perfect (Matthew 5:48). But what does this mean in practice? For Wesley, Christian perfection was not rigid psychological perfectionism. It does not include every conceivable kind of goodness. It is only perfection in love. If and when we have it, we can and very likely will still be defective in many other ways. We might still be ignorant of many things, make all kinds of practical mistakes, be socially awkward, be sorely tempted, and even do accidental and unintentional harm to others.

Clearly, Methodists *strive* for perfection, but do we ever *achieve* it in this life? This was a matter of great controversy among Wesley and his "Methodist Connexion" ministers and members. Wesley himself thought that a few Christians actually do achieve perfection in love, but usually only on their death beds. Clearly, most of us only strive for it or are trying to "go on to it," as Hebrews 6:1 would say. Commenting on this text, Wesley wrote, "Yes, and when ye have attained a measure of perfect love, when God has . . . enabled you to love him with all your heart and with all your soul, think not of resting there. That is impossible. You cannot stand still; you must either rise or fall—rise higher or fall lower. Therefore the voice of God to the children of Israel, to the children of God is, 'Go forward.'"[7]

As best we can, though imperfectly, we do the "labours of love." "Love cannot be hid any more than light;" Wesley said, "and least of all when it shines forth in action, when ye exercise yourselves in the labour of love, in beneficence of every kind;" so each Christian should be a "holy, zealous, active lover of God and man."[8] The second love commandment is the very heart of Christian ethics, just as the first is the very heart of Christian spirituality. Wesley said,

> And the second commandment is like unto this [the first]; the second great branch of Christian righteousness is closely and inseparably connected therewith, even 'Thou shalt love thy neighbor as thyself.' 'Thou shalt

love'—thou shalt embrace with the most tender good-will, the most earnest and cordial affection, the most inflamed desires of preventing or removing all evil and of procuring for him every possible good.[9]

Methodists, Wesley explained, are "to do no harm, to do good, [and] to attend to the ordinances of God."[10] "Love is productive of all right actions," he proclaimed, and, it "constrains [all Christians] to do all possible good, of every possible kind, to all men."[11] Almost always, we fall short of living up to these ideals. Most of us only strive toward moral and spiritual perfection with God's help and with the support and encouragement of other members of the body of Christ.

The "all men" words above are very important. Wesley knew that in practice most of us draw the line somewhere when it comes to loving, helping, doing good, and recognizing others as our neighbors with equal worth before God. We are naturally inclined to love, do good to, and grant moral significance only to insiders, only to people like us, only to "our kind of people," but not to outsiders, not to people who are different, not to "those kind of people."

As Wesley spelled this out, we are disposed to love only our friends, relatives, or acquaintances, only good people but not bad ones, only those we have seen but not those unseen, only those who are kind to us but not those who despitefully use us, only those who express gratitude to us but not the "froward, the evil and unthankful," only those in our own place and nation but not others elsewhere, only those of our own political party but not those in other parties.[12] (We might add that God even loves the politicians we can't stand, but God expects more loving policies and behaviors from them than they usually give. So should we.) The real Christian "loves every soul that God has made, every child of man, of whatever place or nation."[13] Wesley did not mention skin color in this particular context, but many professed Christians today, still do not recognize members of other races (or religions) as our "neighbors." All human prejudices exclude others who God loves and regards as our neighbors.

Wesley's Own Loving Works

John Wesley practiced what he preached. Usually. He did everything he could to help people of all social classes, especially the poor, live better lives here and now. He taught, "It is his [God's] will that we should be inwardly and outwardly holy; that we should be good and do good in every kind, and in the highest degree whereof we are capable."[14] We cannot tell the whole story of Wesley's own good works here, but let's consider a few high points.

Wesley insisted on and provided for the education of his lay preachers, as we saw earlier. His Methodist classes, bands, Sunday schools, and societies educated their lay members, often starting from scratch by teaching illiterate adults how to read, write, and do arithmetic. Schools for children were created and financed. Basic education skills, he thought, did more than just empower people to read the Bible and the books in his Christian Library. Adequate and accurate information has great practical significance for living better, more prosperously, more effectively, and more meaningfully, day to day—at home, at play, on the job, and at rest.

Wesley offered much good practical advice and useful information about managing daily personal and business affairs. Yes, Jesus banned laying up treasures on earth, but first, Wesley explained, he did not forbid us to pay the debts we owe to others. More importantly,

> Neither, secondly, does he here forbid the providing for ourselves such things as are needful for the body; a sufficiency of plain, wholesome food to eat, and clean raiment to put on. Yea, it is our duty, so far as God puts it into our power, to provide these things also; to the end that we may 'eat our own bread,' and be 'burdensome to no man'.
>
> Nor yet are we forbidden, thirdly, to provide for our children and for those of our own household. This also it is our duty to do, even upon principles of heathen morality. Every man ought to provide the plain necessaries of life both for his own wife and children, and to put them into a capacity of providing these for themselves, when he is gone and hence is no more seen. I say, of providing these, the plain necessaries of life-not delicacies, not superfluities-and that by their diligent labour; for it is no man's duty to furnish them, any more than by himself, with the means either of luxury or idleness.
>
> Lastly, we are not forbidden in these words to lay up, from time to time what is needful for carrying on our worldly business in such a measure and degree as is sufficient to answer the foregoing purposes.[15]

Wesley was not against business or money. He agreed with I Timothy 6:10 that not money itself, but the love of money, is "the root of all evil" (though not literally of *all* evil, as we now know).[16] Money itself "is an excellent gift of God, answering the noblest ends."[17] To help others, we must have the resources required for helping. Usually, we must earn them, though some people inherit great wealth. (Today, some people even win the lot- tery and think they are especially blessed by God!).

Sometimes, people have to borrow money for business and peronal purposes. Wesley begged enough money to fund it, then established a lending fund somewhere around 1747 that made small business loans to poor people who could not borrow funds elsewhere. This fund helped hundreds of people get started with or continue with small business ventures.

In his sermon on "The Use of Money," Wesley gave three rules for "the right use of money." First, "Gain all you can" through "honest industry" and by "using in your business all the understanding which God has given you," but without harming your own or anyone else's mind, body, or soul.[18] Second, "Save all you can." This means don't live for costly and foolish desires and pleasures. Don't live wastefully and extravagantly. Don't try to impress people with your wealth. (We might call this "conspicuous consumption.") And don't try to leave a large inheritance for your children.[19] Third, Wesley advised, "Give all you can," as a faithful and sacrificing steward of all that God has given to you.[20]

Methodists began to prosper as the 18th Century progressed, and Wesley suspected in his later years that they were gaining and saving all they could, but not giving all they could.[21]

Wesley had his own version of the "Protestant work ethic." However, he did not agree with Adam Smith, his contemporary, that if everyone acts exclusively from self-interest in business matters, some "invisible hand" will insure that everyone prospers. This theory of economics prevails even today in the corporate world, in business courses and colleges, and in much politics, but Wesley would object strongly to it because it fails to say, "Give all you can." Wesley was persuaded that usually God's hands in the world are our hands, and if God's work in the world is to be done, we have to do it, not some fictitious "invisible hand." This includes helping "the least of these" when they are in great need. He said, "God only changes hearts, yet he generally doeth it by man,"[22] and "It is

God alone who can cast out Satan. But he is generally pleased to do this by man, as an instrument in his hand."[23] If something really needs to be done, most of the time God expects us to do it!

To help people live better lives here and now, Wesley also focused intensely on issues of health. At Oxford, members of the Holy Club visited the poor, sick, widowed, orphaned, and imprisoned, helped them as best they could both physically and spiritually, and offered them self-respect and hope of personal salvation. Later in London and Bristol, Wesley established the first free health clinics ever made available anywhere—"Wesleycare," we might say!

Wesley actually treated patients in those clinics himself. Medicine was not a well-established or well-regulated profession in his day. He wrote that he had read all the books on medical treatments and diagnoses he could get his hands on ever since he was a student at Oxford. By the time his first free clinic opened in London in 1747, he believed himself to be as well prepared to treat patients and to practice medicine as those who set themselves up as medical doctors. Besides, they charged such high fees for their services that poor people could not afford them. He and his generous and giving Methodists could do better by offering free medical clinics, at least for a time.

Wesley taught people sanitation practices for reasons of health. "Cleanliness is indeed next to godliness,"[24] he wrote. He gave instructions on how to eat a healthier diet. He did not consistently practice or commend vegetarianism, but part of the time he was a vegetarian. He wrote that since he quit eating animal flesh, "I have been free (blessed be God) from all bodily disorders."[25] He promoted regular exercise, breathing healthy air, getting a good night's sleep, and otherwise taking care of our bodies. Our bodies are good, not bad, he insisted. They are precious gifts from God, instruments for the use of our souls and for getting God's work done in the world. They are not prisons of our souls, as some philosophers supposed. We should take good care of our very valuable bodies for our own sakes, and so we can help others and avoid being a burden to others. We always use our bodies when we do good and when we actively avoid and prevent evils. We should highly value our own bodies and all of the desirable physical things of the world, but without overvaluing them (as most people do).

To live well, be healthy, provide for our families, and prosper here and now, we must avoid alcohol, Wesley insisted. Alcoholism and drunkenness were prevalent in Wesley's day, especially among the lower and poorer social classes. They used alcohol to escape from their desperate and meaningless lives, just as people do today with alcohol and other drugs. They often spent most of their earnings on alcohol, to the neglect and destitution of their families. Vast quantities of grain were then being used to make alcohol. Wesley thought that this drove up the price of bread so high that poor people could not afford to buy it. Wesley's "Rules" required all Methodists "To taste of no spirituous liquor, no dram of any kind, unless prescribed by a physician."[26] To this day the "Social Principles" of Methodism strongly encourage abstinence from alcohol, harmful drugs, and tobacco.

Wesley did recognize some legitimate medical uses of alcohol, and he prescribed small quantities of beer for various ailments in his own *Primitive Physick*. For the most part, though, Methodists were to be teetotalers. Alcohol ruined lives then, and it still does today. So also do today's so-called "recreational" drugs. Recreation is not a bad thing, but self-destruction is. Is there a viable middle ground between over and under consumption of alcohol?

Wesley wrote and published a cheap book on medical treatments. It was intended for use mainly by poor people who could not afford the services of regular medical doctors. Titled *Primitive Physick, or An Easy and Natural Method of Curing Most Diseases,* it was published in inexpensive paperback form. It was the best-selling book that he ever wrote. First published in 1747, it went through many editions, revisions, and improvements during his lifetime. It stayed in print and in use for many decades after his death. Most of its prescribed treatments would seem to us today as little more than questionable home remedies, but in his day the whole practice of medicine had moved very little beyond that. Keep in mind that home remedies often worked! But not always. Representative of his treatments were:

- For Baldness—"Rub the Part Morning and Evening with *Onions,* 'til it is red; and rub it afterwards with *Honey.*"[27]
- For an Intestinal problem, "Hold a live Puppy constantly on the Belly."[28]
- For Bleeding at the Nose, "Eat raisins much."[29]

Many of the treatments he described were actually quite effective. Wesley was fascinated by electricity. He pioneered its use for many localized afflictions and pains, psychiatric issues, and other medical disorders. He owned four or five electricity machines—small devices that generate a current when a little handle is turned. In his clinic he applied their output to parts of the body that were painful or not functioning properly, even to the head (brain) for mental problems. His own personally tested treatment "For Lunacy" was: "Electrify."[30] One special remedy for both physical and mental ailments, he said, is "far superior to all the other medicines I have known; I mean electricity."[31]

Wesley consistently did all that he could to help poor people, widows, orphans, prisoners, the aged and sick, and anyone else in need. He encouraged all Methodists to follow his example and the example of Christ in such matters. He accomplished so much because so many ordinary Methodists supported and participated in his many "social gospel" projects.

In many ways, Wesley did all he could to make human lives better here and now. For its duration, this life matters greatly, Wesley thought, as does the next. Salvation and the Kingdom of God are with us today, as well as in the future. Things should be on earth as they are in heaven. Our tasks are to pray for this and to help make it so. Usually, God's hands on earth are our hands.

The Faith that Grows: Salvation and Sanctification

A few years ago, a television evangelist was preaching a sermon on growing in grace, and he said, "When you got saved, you didn't get it all." Wesley would have agreed wholeheartedly! Growth in grace and working out our salvation are very important themes in Wesleyan theology. They take a whole lifetime.

When and how do we begin to be Christians? Wesley's principal model for "conversion" was based on his experiences as a Great Awakening evangelist. During protestant revival meetings, then and later, many people had dramatic conversion experiences that they could clearly remember for the rest of their lives. Wesley regarded these transforming experiences as being "born again." New birth involves momentous changes within and without. It both fulfills and transforms who a person really is. New Christians no longer think, believe, feel, choose, or act as they once did. Personal values, beliefs, and practices are clarified and profoundly reordered. But usually everything doesn't happen all at once.

New converts begin by degrees to get their priorities straight. Former objects of love—self alone, worldly prosperity, intellectual idols of the mind—are replaced by the love of God, neighbors, and every creature God has made. The scope of love expands beyond self, kin, kind, party, nation, race, creed, (and sexual orientation?) to include everyone everywhere. Love itself increases immensely in depth, intensity, quality, and scope. Reasoning and knowing abilities improve significantly, as does openness or receptivity to spiritual truths and Christian beliefs. A new sensitivity to the presence of God everywhere—in Christ, in others, and in your own soul—develops. Later if not sooner, the Holy Spirit of God witnesses to your spirit that you are a forgiven, accepted, and beloved child of God. Persisting vices are replaced by growing virtues.

> They know the new birth implies a great change in the soul, in him that is 'born of the Spirit', as was wrought in his body when he was born of a woman; not an outward change only, as from drunkenness to sobriety, from robbery or theft to honesty (this is the poor, dry, miserable conceit of those that know nothing of real religion); but an inward change, from all unholy to all holy tempers, from pride to humility, from passionateness to meekness, from peevishness and discontent to patience and resignation—in a word, from an earthly, sensual, devilish mind to the mind that was in Christ Jesus.[32]

"External" behaviors also change significantly when people become Christians, though usually not all at once. They no longer do sinful things. Instead, they do holy, helpful, and loving things. They no longer nurture and practice their former vices. Instead, they cultivate and practice the Christian virtues. Becoming a truly virtuous person takes a lot of time and practice. One or two good deeds does not make a virtuous person. Developing Christian virtues takes time, effort, and practice. Sanctification, increasing holiness, growth in grace, working out our salvation, are long-term projects. Externally, we must act benevolently and justly so often that they become second nature internally. This is true of all moral and spiritual actions and virtues. Becoming a virtuous Christian involves far more than *occasionally* obeying legalistic rules or commandments. It involves transforming our inner dispositions, desires, feelings, interests, choices, and our external habits. Christian virtue is enduring inward holiness expressed externally in daily living and doing.

Do inner and outer Christian transformations *always* begin with dramatic and memorable "new birth" revival experiences? For a time, while caught up in the Great Awakening, Wesley thought so. Did he ever modify his revivalist model for becoming a Christian? Did he ever recognize that holiness might develop slowly, gradually, and almost imperceptibly? Reluctantly, he did, in due time. He eventually acknowledged that some Methodist Society members were very good Christians even though they never experienced radical and memorable revivalistic conversions. Becoming a Christian can be abrupt and dramatic, but it can also be gradual and almost unnoticeable.

Many if not most Methodist and other Wesleyan churches today no longer stage old-fashioned week-long revival meetings with visiting evangelists and altar calls. Their very good Christian members conform more to a gradual-transformation model than to an abrupt revivalistic-conversion model. In these churches, today's young people just grow up progressively into good Christians with the aid of youth programs, Sunday schools, confirmation classes, regular church attendance, active communal participation in works of mercy and piety, and being surrounded by loving parents, peers, parishioners, church workers, and good moral and spiritual examples. Gradualism prevails today in most of our churches.

Perhaps gradualists experience all of the "new birth" changes that Wesley identified, but more slowly than revival converts. The inner and external moral and spiritual transformations described above really do *start* somewhere, somehow, and somewhen, whether sudden or gradual, but they should not *end* where they begin. Wesley agreed with St. Paul (I. Corinthians 3:2) that all new Christians are only "babes in Christ." All must grow in grace and holiness toward Christian maturity. Some sinfulness may remain in them, (despite his earlier views to the contrary), but it no longer reigns supreme.[33] The initial transformation-marks of true Christians develop and increase throughout the rest of their lives. They are changed, often slowly, from who they once were into a new, higher, and better consciousness, a more Christ-like consciousness. They acquire the minds, the loves, and the actions of Christ. All things become new. But this takes time.

Lifelong growth in grace and working out one's salvation is what Wesley called "sanctification," (saint-making). For the rest of their lives, newborn "babes in Christ" strive to increase their knowledge of and love for God and all of God's creatures. They know from personal experience that "When you got saved, you didn't get it all," as the televangelist put it. New Christians are far from being mature adult Christians. Salvation-justification by faith may or may not be instantaneous, but lifelong sanctification (moral and spiritual growth) begins somewhere, and its transformations are inseparable from saving faith. Sanctification actually takes forever. Spiritual and moral growth are lifelong and even continue after death, Wesley thought. Spiritual maturity is a matter of degree, as is faith itself. What he called "entire sanctification," (perfection in love) is a distant goal for most of us. Some "holiness" Wesleyan churches still emphasize it, as did Wesley himself at times.

Moral and spiritual maturity and perfection in love do not happen overnight. Wesley anticipated lifelong growth toward Christian holiness and perfection: "From the time of our being 'born again' the gradual work of sanctification takes place."[34] Does anyone ever grow into completely mature and perfect love? The most advanced saints approximate it and all the changes that go along with it. For most of us, however, perfect love and Christian maturity are distant, guiding, and luring lights at the end of a very long tunnel of lifetime travel. God still loves, forgives, and saves us, even with our lingering imperfections, that is, "while we are yet sinners."

Today, as in Wesley's day, many Christians seem to think that that only two things of importance ever happen in the lives of Christians. First, they "get saved" by accepting Jesus "as their personal Lord and Savior." Second, they die and go to heaven with a free ticket. And that's it. Salvation means getting a free ticket to heaven, nothing more; nothing spiritually significant ever happens between conversion and death.

Wesley's opinion of this popular view was very negative. He firmly believed that many things of great spiritual significance can and should happen between conversion and death. Holiness happens. "And when we say, 'Believe, and thou shalt be saved,' we do not mean, 'Believe, and thou shalt step from sin to heaven, without any holiness coming between."[35] Wesley totally rejected the idea that salvation has no spiritual impact upon daily Christian living. What happens between conversion and death (most of life itself) is of the utmost moral and spiritual significance. As he explained,

> The salvation which is here spoken of is not what is frequently understood by that word, the going to heaven, eternal happiness. It is not the soul's going to paradise, termed by our Lord, 'Abraham's bosom'. It is not a blessing which lies on the other side of death, or (as we usually speak) in the other world. The very words of the text itself [Ephesians 2:8] put this beyond all question. 'Ye are saved.' It is not something at a distance: it is a present thing, a blessing which, through the free mercy of God, ye are now in possession of. [36]

Salvation is much more than just getting a free ticked to Heaven by and by. It is something we have now; salvation is *today*. It makes a great moral and spiritual difference today, tomorrow, and for the rest of our lives. Our basic values and capacities for valuing gradually but greatly improve. If Christian beginnings are not followed by lifelong growth in grace, love, justice, faith, hope, forgiveness, moral goodness, and spiritual holiness, something very serious has gone wrong. "Unless they have new senses, ideas, passions, tempers, they are no Christians!"[37] Spiritual changes may take a lifetime, and they affect the whole of life. New Christians have new futures. All things become new. Desirable changes, both personal and social, are welcomed and expected. All along, God gives us courage, strength, insight, love, and grace to deal with things predictable, and with those that are unpredictable.

Notes

1. Wesley, "Upon Our Lord's Sermon on the Mount, V" *Works*, 1, 559-560.
2. Wesley, "Of True Christian Faith," Outler, 129.
3. Wesley, "Cautions and Directions Given to the Greatest Professors in the Methodist Societies," Outler, 303.
4. Wesley, "On Zeal," *Works*, 3, 313.
5. Ibid.
6. Ibid.

7. Wesley, "On Faith: Hebrews 11:6," *Works*, 3, 501.

8. Wesley, "Upon Our Lord's Sermon on the Mount, IV," *Works*, 1, 539-540.

9. Wesley, "The Way to the Kingdom," *Works*, 1, 221.

10. Wesley, "Upon Our Lord's Sermon on the Mount, V," *Works*, 1, 568 and further explained on 569-571. See also Wesley, "General Rules of the United Societies," *Works*, 9, 70-73.

11. Wesley, "A Plain Account of Genuine Christianity," Outler, 185.

12. Wesley, "The Way to the Kingdom," *Works*, 1, 221-222

13. Ibid., 1, 222; Wesley, "A Plain Account of Genuine Christianity," Outler, 184.

14. Wesley, "The Nature of Enthusiasm," *Works*, 2, 54-55.

15. Wesley, "Upon Our Lord's Sermon on the Mount, VIII," *Works*, 1, 618-619.

16. Wesley, "Upon Our Lord's Sermon on the Mount, I," *Works*, 1, 476.

17. Wesley, "The Use of Money," *Works*, 2, 268.

18. Ibid., *Works*, 2, 268-273.

19. Ibid., *Works*, 2, 273-276.

20. Ibid., *Works*, 2, 277-280.

21. Wesley, "The Danger of Riches," *Works*, 3, 236-246,

22. Wesley, "Upon Our Lord's Sermon on the Mount, IV," *Works*, 1, 546.

23. Wesley, "A Caution against Bigotry," *Works*, 2, 68.

24. Wesley, "On Dress," *Works*, 3, 249.

25. Wesley, "Letter to Dr. Gibson, Bishop of London," June 11, 1747.

26. Wesley, "Directions given to the Band Societies," Dec. 25, 1744," *Works*, 9, 79.

27. John Wesley, *Primitive Physick, or An Easy and Natural Method of Curing Most Diseases,* London: W. Strahan, 1761, 36.

28. Ibid., 76.

29. Ibid., 36.

30. Ibid., 81.

31. Ibid., xxvii.

32. Wesley, "On God's Vineyard," *Works*, 3, 506.

33. Wesley, "On Sin in Believers," *Works*, 1, 327, 321 and note 32.

34. Wesley, "The Scripture Way of Salvation," *Works*, 2, 160.

35. Wesley, "Upon Our Lord's Sermon on the Mount, V," *Works*, 1, 560.

36. Wesley, "The Scripture Way of Salvation," *Works*, 2, 156

37. Wesley, "On Living without God," *Works*, 4, 174-175.

CHAPTER 6

OTHER CHRISTIANS AND OTHER FAITHS

As Wesley knew, we are naturally disposed not to love or respect those who differ from ourselves in beliefs or practices, religious or otherwise. He knew that Christians differ considerably in both fundamental and marginal beliefs, as well as in devotional and cultural practices. He knew that our differences are especially great with respect to persons of other religious faiths and persuasions. He gave such differences much serious thought. What he said about such things back then can be very illuminating and helpful to us today.

Diverse Christian Practices

Have you ever heard anyone say, "It really doesn't matter what you believe as long as your heart is in the right place"? Many Wesleyans think this way and say these words with respect to our relations with Christians of other denominations, faiths, and practices. Others may or may not think this way about us, but this is how we think about them. That other Christians have different beliefs and practices troubled Wesley, as it should us. He searched earnestly for what all Christians have in common. He expressed his conclusions in his sermon on Catholic Christianity titled "Catholic Spirit," where "catholic" meant "universal," not "Roman Catholic." What do Christians have in common everywhere? That was his question. What was his answer?

Different denominations have different practices, Wesley acknowledged, and all insist that only their own way is "scriptural and apostolic." Finding catholic or universal Christianity in devotional practices or organizational structures is difficult, maybe impossible. Some churches have episcopal governments with bishops while others favor local congregational control. Some practice infant baptism; some don't. Some use formal written prayers, but others prefer more spontaneous "extemporary" prayers. Some use lay preachers; some don't. Some immerse in baptism, some sprinkle, some pour.[1] Wesley noted that Christians also differ greatly in "indifferent" things like apparel, body postures, meats and drinks, covering heads, and abstaining from marriage.[2] These are not always regarded as indifferent!

We could easily expand Wesley's lists of diverse Christian devotional practices, Works of Piety, and means of grace much further that he did. Wesley's own list of Works of Piety seems to have been very open-ended. As we know, some churches allow musical instruments like pianos, organs, and guitars; some do not. Some wash feet or speak in tongues; most do not. Would Wesley have recognized these devotional practices as legitimate Works of Piety and effective means of grace for some, even if not for all? Probably so. Some churches do not require baptism for church membership; most do. Christians probably used real wine in the Lord's Supper in Wesley's day. Most still do today, but we Methodist now use unfermented pasteurized grape juice.

Methodists have a long history of participation in the Temperance Movement. This dates back to Wesley's nearly absolute prohibition of alcohol. In the late 1800s, some Methodists squeezed fresh grape juice shortly before Communion Sunday to avoid serving alcohol, but that was not very easy or practical. Some even substituted water for wine, since Jesus turned water into wine. The problem of not using alcohol in communion wine was solved for us in 1869 when a Methodist layman, a former preacher named Thomas B. Welch, discovered how to pasteurize grape juice to keep it from fermenting. He gradually marketed it. "Welch's Grape Juice" slowly but steadily came into use at Methodist communion services. You can buy it today in your local grocery store. A Methodist General Conference in 1880 made such unfermented grape juice all but mandatory.

Clearly, Christian practices are very diverse, probably too diverse for finding universals. But what about Christian beliefs?

Diverse Christian Beliefs

Wesley was also greatly concerned about Christian disagreements over beliefs or doctrines. As with practices, each denomination views only its own beliefs as truly scriptural and apostolic. Predestination is a good example of this. Most Catholics and Protestants before Wesley accepted and taught it, but Wesley and his Methodists rejected it. Both sides could quote scripture.

The close evangelical and personal relationship between John Wesley and George Whitefield ultimately came to an end over predestination, though they tried their best to remain friends. Whitefield ultimately established his own Calvinistic Methodist Church. It survives today as the Presbyterian Church of Wales. Wesley fought constantly against predestination, and Whitefield fought constantly for it. When Whitefield died in 1770, Wesley was invited to preach his funeral sermon. He did so without mentioning predestination.

You have heard the expression, "agree to disagree." John Wesley was the first person ever to use this exact expression *in print*, but he did *not* claim to have *originated* it. He gave George Whitefield credit for that. Whitefield and Wesley finally agreed to disagree about predestination while remaining friends, somewhat estranged. Christians often arrive at that kind of a truce with other Christians over many debatable issues, some very serious and unfriendly.

In Wesley's own words, Methodists "think and let think," with respect to "beliefs that do not strike at the root of Christianity."[3] But what beliefs *are* at the root of Christianity? Even here, we disagree, as did the apostles themselves.[4] Wesley identified them as "God is love," the two love Commandments, and any additional beliefs and practices that illustrate, support, nurture, encourage, or express love, goodness, and devotion. Such Christian beliefs might include the incarnation, the life and teachings of Christ, his atonement for our sins, his resurrection, the gift and presence of the Holy Spirit, and many others. All express and manifest God's love for us. Of course, what works lovingly for some may not work for others.

Many existing Christian beliefs and practices actually have little bearing, if any, on God as love, being loved by God, and loving God and our neighbors. Many existing Christian beliefs are quite irrelevant to living a life of love. Some may even interfere with living lovingly. Wesley advised, "Do not spend your time and strength contending for or against such things as of a disputable nature;" instead leave "a thousand disputable points to those who have no better business than to toss the ball of controversy to and fro."⁵

Spiritually and morally, many religious disputes, he thought, are just a waste of time. Many such beliefs are really not worth worrying about. We may be intellectually curious about them, but we should not expect the time and effort we spend on them to help us grow in grace, holiness, virtue, and love. What are our divinity schools now teaching? Do they concentrate primarily on those spiritual and moral concerns likely to contribute to the sanctification and moral integrity of divinity students and their eventual parishioners? Is much of a divinity school education largely irrelevant to what ministers must say and do once they are out "in the field"?

In today's small world, how should we relate to other Christians who think and practice differently? Wesley advised,

> Condemn no man for not thinking as you think. Let every man use his own judgment, since every man must give an account of himself to God. Abhor every reproach, in any kind or degree, to the spirit of *persecution*. If you cannot *reason* or *persuade* a man into the truth, never attempt to *force* him into it. If love will not compel him to come in, leave him to God, the Judge of all.⁶

So, what was Wesley's answer to his own question about catholic or universal Christianity? What, if anything, do all Christians have in common, despite their differences? He definitely rejected, "Embrace my modes of worship [and beliefs] or I will embrace yours;" and he acknowledged, "We must both act [and believe] as each is fully persuaded in his own mind. Hold you fast that which you believe is most acceptable to God, and I will do the same."⁷ Thus, Wesley's best and enduring advice would be: You do your thing, and I will do mine! As long as we do it lovingly! Love is what we all have in common.

Universal Christianity cannot be found in either theological "opinions" or devotional and administrative practices. Wesley did dispute about them, reluctantly. What helps some people become more loving might not work for others. Universal Christianity is a matter of the heart, not of the head, not of worship practices, and not of church organization. It all boils down to love. "'If thine heart is as my heart.' If thou lovest God and all mankind, I ask no more: 'Give me thine hand.'"[8] That was Wesley's definitive answer. Love is what all Christians have in common, (at least ideally).

And how are we today to decide personally about what to believe and practice religiously? In the spirit of John Wesley, we should ask of every spiritual belief and practice: "Will this help me to become a more loving person? Or less? Or will it make no difference at all?" Finally, we just have to make up our own minds in the spirit of love, given the "best light" available to us. To everyone trying to assess the truth or falsity of "opinions," Wesley said, "Judge for yourselves by the best light you have."[9]

An enlightened faith and a blind faith are very different. Wesley wanted an enlightened faith for himself and for all Methodists. An enlightened faith is all that we can ever expect from any intelligent and well informed approach to religion (or to anything else). Wesley advised Christian seekers to "act [and believe] according to the light you have."[10] The brightest and most reliable spiritual light available to anyone, no matter what they believe or practice, is the light of love. This applies to both non-Christians and Christians. Wesley's words were, "I regard even faith not as an end but a means only. The end of the commandment is love, of every command, of the whole Christian dispensation. *Let this love be attained, by whatever means*, and I am content; I desire no more. All is well, if we love the Lord our God with all our heart and our neighbor as ourselves."[11]

Non-Christian Beliefs and Practices

Is "all well" with loving persons who are not Christians? How Christians should think about, feel about, and act toward non-Christians is one of today's most urgent concerns. We live in a very small world. Those of other faiths now live very close to us and all around us. We are in prolonged wars with far too many of them. Wesley thought very seriously about our relations with non-Christians. What he concluded was very insightful and can be very helpful to us.

Wesley's knowledge of non-Christian religions was somewhat limited. He was at best somewhat acquainted with Judaism and Islam. He knew very little about the religions of the Far East like Hinduism, Buddhism, Taoism, and Shintoism, but he was an avid reader of, and did learn something about them from, missionary reports and travel-logs. What he said about Judaism, Islam, and "heathenism" in general can be readily extended to all world religions.

Wesley was definitely not a Christian exclusivist. Exclusivists insist that the only way to be "saved" is to believe in Jesus, and this consigns all people in non-Christian ages and places to Hell, especially if "believing" means affirming certain doctrines about Jesus. About Jews, Muslims, and all non-Christians ("heathens"), Wesley had three very significant things to say.

First, God has given us no authority to judge such people, so we should leave that and them entirely to God. As Wesley put it, "I have no authority from the Word of God 'to judge those that are without.' Nor do I conceive that any man living has a right to sentence all the heathen and Mahometan world to damnation. It is far better to leave them to him that made them, and who is 'the Father of the spirits of all flesh'; who is the God of the heathens as well as the Christians, and who hateth nothing that he hath made."[12] According to Wesley, "He that believeth not shall be damned" (Mark 16:16) applies only to "them to whom the gospel is preached. Others it does not concern; and we are not required to determine anything touching their final state. How it will please God, the Judge of all, to deal with them we may leave to God himself."[13] As for "our modern Jews, . . . it is not our part to pass sentence upon them, but to leave them to their own Master."[14]

Second, all persons, all non-Christians, who live up to the best light they have will be saved and are acceptable to God. As Wesley explained, "But this we know, that he is not the God of the Christians only, but the God of the heathens also; that he is 'rich in mercy to all that call upon him' [Romans 10:12], 'according to the light they have' [Romans 12:6]; and that 'in every nation he that feareth God and worketh righteousness is accepted of him [Acts 10:35]."[15] Wesley considered and rejected exclusivism more than once. Elsewhere he wrote,

> But in every nation he that feareth God and worketh righteousness – He that, first, reverences God, as great, wise, good, the cause, end, and governor of all things; and secondly, from this awful regard to him, not only avoids all known evil, but endeavours, according to the best light he has, to do

all things well; is accepted of him – Through Christ, though he knows him not. The assertion is express, and admits of no exception. He is in the favour of God, whether enjoying his written word and ordinances or not.[16]

Through Christ, all the good, holy, faithful, loving, and practicing people we read about in the Old Testament were also "partakers of the same salvation"[17] if they lived by the best light they had, even though they knew nothing about Jesus and had no beliefs about him. Many non-Christians really have lived up to their own best light, and "Their not believing the whole truth is not owing to want of sincerity, but merely to want of light."[18] Even without the light of distinctively Christian beliefs, they were fully acceptable to God.

The third important thing that Wesley said about non-Christians is also to be found in the above quotes. Namely, the love and goodness of God, and the redemptive work of Christ, are sufficiently powerful to save and restore *everyone everywhere of all faiths* as long as they live by the best light they have. Each person is made acceptable to God "Through Christ though he knows him not." Of course, only Christians would accept the "redemptive work of Christ" part of this third point. But Wesley definitely thought that even without any knowledge of the Christian revelation, non-Christians can still have "true religion." He read a book by an Arabian "Mahometan" author and proclaimed that it "contains all the principles of pure religion pure and undefiled."[19] Yet, nothing in this book affirmed distinctly Christian "opinions" about Jesus.

In Wesley's 18th Century England and Europe, ignorance of, misconceptions about, and prejudices toward Muslims and Jews were almost universal, even among the most educated. Seen against this background, Wesley's views were quite remarkable. Some people even today may find them quite astounding! *Universal* love itself is quite astounding! To Christian exclusivists who deny universal love, Wesley would say, God "hateth nothing that he hath made."

One serious problem remains for us that Wesley may not have resolved. How do his three points apply to *those within* "the Christian dispensation" who reject Christian theism and orthodoxy? In all intellectual honesty, and after much soul-searching, many who have been adequately exposed to Christian preaching and biblical revelation cannot affirm what Christians believe. Wesley applied his three points above only those who do *not* fall within "the Christian dispensation." But what of *those within* who self-consciously and in all honesty reject most Christian beliefs, yet they are morally good, loving, and open- minded people living up to the best light they have? Are we authorized by God to judge them? Does the God who hates nothing he has made actually hate them? Are the love and goodness of God and the redemptive work of Christ not sufficiently powerful to save and restore them, even if they do not assent to the "opinions" of Christian orthodoxy? To repeat, Wesley wrote, "The end of the commandment is love, of every command, of the whole Christian dispensation. Let this love be attained, by whatever means, and I am content; I desire no more." [20] Why shouldn't this apply to honest but loving doubters within Christendom? Who could ask anything more of anyone?

Wesley's remarkable understanding of "prevenient grace" can also illuminate our own approach to non-Christians. He affirmed the traditional doctrine of "original sin" on both biblical and experiential grounds. This doctrine says that all people are disposed by nature to desire and do unloving, unjust, immoral, and irreligious things. Because of its prevalence, most human image of God capacities have been lost, greatly diminished, or never developed. Our abilities to reason, love the right things, sense God's presence, know the difference between right and wrong, grow in grace, and become aware of our personal sinfulness, are greatly diminished or underdeveloped because of our inner propensities toward sin. By nature, we are disposed toward tribalism, bullying, ignorance, confusion, superficiality, selfishness, loving the wrong things, fascination with nonstop distractions, insensitivity to the presence of God, and diminished conscience. We are oblivious to or content with our own evil-doing, evil-thinking, and evil feelings and dispositions.

So just how greatly diminished are we in our original "state of nature"? Are we *totally* depraved and destitute morally and spiritually, as Luther and other protestant thinkers held? Or are we only *greatly* so, as most Catholic thinkers believed? Wesley did affirm the Protestant doctrine of "total depravity," *but always with the qualification* that this is how things would were it not for God's *prevenient grace*, available to all. Wesley's discussion of "natural man" with no goodness at all in him (or her) was qualified by "We are not here to consider what the grace of God might occasionally work in his soul."[21]

According to Wesley, "There is no man that is in a state of mere nature," because of God's prevenient or "preventing" grace.[22] Every person, of every religion, in every place and time, has some degree of the grace and image of God—a working conscience, good desires, love, compassion, a rational mind, and "some measure of that light, some faint glimmering ray, which sooner or later, more or less, enlightens every man that cometh into the world."[23] Saint Paul said that even the Gentiles do [and know] by nature (or conscience) what the moral law requires (Romans 2:14-15), and Wesley agreed.[24] Prevenient grace gives some light to all, and God accepts everyone who lives up to the best light she or he has. Prevenient grace may even enable us today to celebrate and rejoice in our religious differences, respect one another, love one another, and learn from one another. Those of other faiths are also our "neighbors," to be loved as we love ourselves. Yes, we are to love our own personal enemies, but even God's enemies, are to be so loved.[25]

Lutherans, Calvinists, and others may do this, but Wesleyans can never make a sharp distinction between what the world and its people are like *without* God's grace, as opposed to *with* God's grace. No world and no people ever exist without a significant degree of God prevenient grace and universal love.

Notes

1. Wesley, "Catholic Spirit," *Works*, 2, 90.
2. Wesley, "The Character of a Methodist," *Works*, 9, 34.
3. Ibid.
4. Wesley, "A Caution against Bigotry," *Works*, 2, 70.
5. Wesley, "On Attending the Church Service," *Works*, 3, 478.
6. Wesley, "Advice to a People Called Methodists," *Works*, 9, 130.
7. Wesley, "Catholic Spirit," *Works*, 2, 90.
8. Wesley's text for "Catholic Spirit" was 2 Kings, 10:15.
9. Wesley, "A Farther Appeal to Men of Reason and Religion, Part II," *Works*, 11, 203-204.
10. Wesley, "Catholic Spirit," *Works*, 2, 90.

11. Wesley, "To John Smith," June 25, 1746, *Works*, 26, 206. Italics added.
12. Wesley, "On Living without God," *Works*, 4, 174.
13. Wesley, "On Charity," *Works*, 3, 295-296.
14. Wesley, "On Faith: Hebrews 11:6," *Works*, 3, 495.
15. Wesley, "On Charity," *Works*, 3, 296.
16. Wesley, *Explanatory Notes Upon the New Testament*, Acts 10:35.
17. Wesley, "The Mystery of Iniquity," *Works*, 2, 452-453.
18. Wesley, "On Faith: Hebrews 11:6," *Works*, 3, 494.
19. Ibid., 494-495.
20. Wesley, "To John Smith," June 25, 2007, section 9, Jackson, *Works*, 26.
21. Wesley, "Original Sin," *Works*, 2, 175.
22. Wesley, "On Working Out Our Own Salvation," *Works*, 3, 207.
23. Ibid.
24. See Wesley's comments on these verses in his *Explanatory Notes Upon the New Testament*.
25. Wesley, "Catholic Spirit," *Works*, 2, 89, Wesley, "The Character of a Methodist," *Works*, 9, 38, Wesley, "The Reformation of Manners," *Works*, 2, 321.

Chapter 7

People and Animals in the Image of God

The *Imago Dei*, the image of God in human beings, looms large in Christian theology, including Wesley's. Do you know where the Bible says that human beings, both male and female, were created in the image of God? Answer: Genesis 1. And do you know exactly what this image or likeness is according to Genesis 1? Answer: This is a trick question. The first chapter of Genesis never says exactly what that image is. Neither does the rest of the Old Testament.

One verse, Colossians 4:24 in the New Testament, suggests that the image of God within us might be *knowledge*, but that is not the answer given by most Christian theologians through the centuries. Theologians, then and now, actually identify that quality or capacity within us that they value the most, and then they call that "God's image" within us. Every traditional answer to, "What exactly is that image?" goes beyond both Genesis 1 and Colossians 4:24, as we will see. There is no definitive biblical answer. Still, this is a very important, enlightened, and inspiring Christian belief. Before reading any further, ask yourself what *you* think the image of God is within us, and discuss this with others if possible.

People in the Image of God

Almost every Christian thinker who lived before Wesley gave the same answer. The image of God in us is *Reason or Intelligence*, they said. This is a Greek philosophical answer, not a biblical answer. "Knowledge," as in Colossians 4:24, can come to us in many ways in addition to reason, for example, through experience, conscience, or revelation, so this is not the same thing as "reason." Even the heart has its reasons. And just what reason is and how it works has always been a matter of controversy, even among those firmly committed to "reason alone." Wesley has his own understanding of what reason is and how it works, as we saw earlier.

Early in the 2nd Century CE, Jewish and Christian thinkers began to read the Greek philosophers and to interpret their Hebraic scriptures and convictions using notions, beliefs, and ways of thinking taken from Greek philosophy. Reason was the human capacity valued most by ancient Greek philosophers. Very early and then thereafter, Christian thinkers greatly influenced by the Greek philosophers guessed that reason is the image of God within us. St. Thomas Aquinas, who is still the official philosopher of the Roman Catholic Church, put it this way, "Man is said to be in the image of God, not as regards his body, but as regards that whereby he excels other animals . . . Now man excels all animals by his reason and intellect; hence it is according to his intellect and reason, which are incorporeal, that man is said to be in the image of God."[1] This answer was based on Aristotle's definition of "man" as a "rational animal." The Aristotelian view is that "reason" is the obvious difference between "us" and "them." We have it; they don't.

Wesley's own theory of the image of God within us illustrates how creative, progressive, and downright radical his theological thinking often was. His predecessors for the most part gave a very simple answer. Reason is that image. Wesley gave a much more complex answer. He greatly valued *many* of our Godlike capabilities, not just one. He distinguished between the "natural" image of God and the "moral" image of God within us. Sometimes he added the "political" image of God.

In explaining *the natural image of God* within us, Wesley identified at least four significant divine/human similarities (sometimes five). He wrote, "For he [God] created man in his own image: a spirit like himself; a spirit endued with understanding, with will or affections, and liberty."[2] Like God, we are 1. spirits (immaterial souls), endowed with 2. reason or understanding, 3. will (desires, feelings, affections), and 4. liberty or freedom of choice. But what do these mean?

1. God's being a *spirit* indicates that God has no body. Jesus said that God is a spirit (John 4:24), but he did not explain what he meant by that. After Greek philosophical ideas were applied to biblical religion, being a "spirit" then meant being "immaterial," or "incorporeal," that is, hav-

ing no body, no physical qualities and relations at all. Unlike bodies, spirits have no spatial qualities like size, shape, weight, movement, position, color, etc. They have only psychological qualities, relations, and functions or capacities. Recall Wesley's insistence that we cannot take literally any physical imagery (like hands, face, eyes, sides, etc.) when applied to God in the Bible. He said that "[M]an was made in God's image, and after his likeness; two words to express the same thing. God's image upon man, consists, in his nature, not that of his body, for God has not a body, but that of his soul. The soul is a spirit, an intelligent, immortal spirit, an active spirit, herein resembling God, the Father of spirits, and the soul of the world."[3]

Some people think that existing in the image of God means that we look like God, and God looks like us. Vision detects or directly experiences our image of or likeness to God. God is envisioned as a large, distinguished, bearded, white-skinned, humanoid male "in the sky." Michelangelo's magnificent painting on the ceiling of the Sistine Chapel in Rome of God reaching out his hand to Adam well illustrates this understanding—or misunderstanding.

Wesley agreed with practically all earlier Christian thinkers that we definitely do not resemble God physically because God has no body. God is an immaterial disembodied spirit. Our souls are also immaterial spirits, but we are embodied; we are "clothed with a material vehicle."[4] God is totally unembodied, unclothed, even though God is "the soul of the world." So, does God look like us? Do we look like God? No. God has no looks.

Present day process thinkers suggest that the world, the universe, (or some world if God has created other universes) is the body of God, but that is not exactly how Wesley understood it. Maybe he should have. Anyhow, the universe is not shaped like a very large male human being.

2. Wesley used *understanding* interchangeably with *reason*. He did not completely dismiss the classical view that reason is the image of God within us. It really is *one* aspect of that image, but it is not the only one. He called it "the most essential property of spirit,"[5] but he added a lot to it. Will, liberty of choice, and conscience are also aspects of God's natural image within us. Reason may be the most essential natural capacity of spirit, but love is our most essential moral/spiritual trait.

3. *Willing* today usually means choosing, but this is not what Wesley

meant by *will*. He equated it with the affective or feeling part of the human soul, not the choosing part. "Man," he explained, "was endued also with a *will*, with various affections (which are only the will exerting itself in various ways) that he might love, desire, and delight in that which is good."[6] All of us have many "affections," some good or desirable, some bad or undesirable. Some are holy, some unholy.

The most important thing about Wesley's understanding of "will" or the "affections" is that this is where love and compassion are located in the human soul. Unlike practically every Christian thinker who came before him, Wesley identified *love* as the most basic feature of the moral and spiritual image of God within us, as it was within Adam and Eve. "In this [*moral*] image of God was man made. 'God is love:' accordingly man at his creation was full of love; which was the sole principle of all his tempers, thoughts, words, and actions. God is full of justice, mercy, and truth: so was man as he came from the hands of his Creator."[7]

4. *Liberty* of choice is another capacity of the human soul. It is very different from will, feelings, and emotions, desires, and the affections. Wesley defended "liberty of choice," but not "free will," as we often call it today. He defined "liberty" as "a power of choosing what was good, and refusing what was not so."[8] Without it, we would not be free and responsible agents. Indeed we would not be agents at all. We would be nothing more than passive patients, disposed and determined in every respect by God. Liberty of choice is our God-given capacity for self-determination, for originating our own choices, for not having all of our decisions programmed into us from eternity by God, and for not being completely determined by anything else within the created world.

In addition to being created in the natural image of God, Wesley thought that human beings, Adam and Eve originally, were also created in the *political image* of God. This meant that God gave human beings dominion or rule over all other living creatures. "Chiefly," however, Adam and Eve were created in the *moral image* of God, that is, as perfect in "righteousness and true holiness"[9] as suggested in Ephesians 4:24. Morality and spirituality were inseparable aspects of this image. In the perfection of Eden, the "understanding" capacity of Adam and Eve was "without blemish." Their evaluations were always "set right, and duly exercised on their proper objects." Their consciences were clear, innocent, accurate, and dependable. They always made the right choices and selected what they knew to be best. They had "uninterrupted fellowship" with God and were "unspeakably happy."[10] These perfections and this bliss were greatly diminished by the fall, Wesley thought. Yet, by God's prevenient grace, lesser degrees of understanding, conscience, self-awareness, desirable affections, love, compassion, a sense of justice, liberty of choice, moral activity, and spiritual sensitivity to God remain in all persons everywhere. With or without Adam and Eve, this is about where we are now.

Animals in the Image of God

Wesley had revolutionary ideas about how Christians should understand and relate in practice to non-human animals. He was convinced that they too 1. are created in the image of God (including reason or understanding), 2. are endowed with anticipations of morality, 3. are loved by God, who is greatly concerned for their happiness and well-being, 4. should be treated by us in accord with God's mercy and the Golden Rule, 5. have immaterial and immortal souls or spirits, and 6. will be present in Heaven (or in the final "New Creation") in a re-embodied state. Most of today's ethics-and-animals advocates would be very proud of John Wesley, considering where and when he lived! Let's begin with the image of God in animals.

1. Wesley believed that by degrees animals have the same *natural* image of God traits and capacities that we human beings have. His most serious thoughts about the proper Christian view of animals were expressed in two of his later sermons, "The General Deliverance," (1782) and "The New Creation," (1785). In the first of these he wrote,

> What was the original state of the brute creatures, when they were first created? This deserves a more attentive consideration than has been usually given it. It is certain these, as well as man, had an innate principle of *self-motion*; and that at least in as high a degree as they enjoy it at this day. Again: they were endued with a degree of *understanding* not less than that they are possessed of now. They had also a *will*, including various passions, which, likewise, they still enjoy. And they had *liberty*, a power of choice; a degree of which is still found in every living creature. Nor can we doubt but their understanding too was in the beginning perfect in

its kind. Their passions and affections were regular, and their choice always guided by their understanding.[11]

Wesley thus ascribed the same natural image of God capacities to animals that we have. In us, these capacities are greatly weakened by sinfulness. Indirectly, the animals were also adversely affected by human sinfulness, he thought. (If we do not take the Adam and Eve story literally, we could still say that these capacities have always been less well developed than they ideally ought to be in both us and the animals.) By God's prevenient grace, none of these capacities were ever "totally depraved" or completely extinguished in either humans or animals. Prevenient grace went into effect the very moment that Adam sinned, Wesley thought.

Wesley begins the above quote with *self-motion*—a fifth aspect of the image of God. Both human beings and animals also have this God-like capacity. Unlike Newtonian matter, which is motionless until it is bumped or pulled by something else, both animals and human beings are self-starters, capable of initiating their own activities. Metaphorically, this can be extended to our psychological as well as to our physical abilities. Wesley did not say in the above quote that animals are spirits, but he had already affirmed that the capacity for self-motion belongs to human beings and to "every spirit in the universe; this being the proper distinguishing difference between spirit and matter."[12] As self-moving, animals are spirits, but they are also much more.

Animals are also endowed with *understanding (reason), will, and liberty of choice*, that is, with all of our natural image of God properties. By degrees, both people and sub-human animals are rational animals—some species and individuals more so than others. Christian thinkers before Wesley assumed that only human beings are created in the image of God, and only human beings are rational. Wesley completely disagreed. The Bible does not tell us exactly what that image is, so Wesley and his predecessors (and successors) usually identified the *image* in non-biblical ways.

An ulterior motive traditionally guided the search for our image of God likeness. Earlier Christian thinkers presumed that if they could find some capacity that belongs exclusively to us but not to sub-human animals, *that* would be the image of God within us. Following the Greek philosophers, they identified *reason* as just that capacity. Aristotle had defined human beings as "rational animals," where rationality is the "faculty" that absolutely distinguishes us from them. Not so, said Wesley!

Wesley was convinced that animals, too, are rational by degrees. Reason is not an absolute difference between us and them. Wesley used "reason" and "understanding" interchangeably. By attributing understanding to animals, Wesley rejected most of the philosophical and theological traditions that came before him. This is one of his truly rebellious and revolutionary ideas. In today's ethics-and-animals discussion, Charles Darwin is usually credited with being the first serious thinker to challenge the traditional view that animals aren't rational, but Wesley beat Darwin to the punch by 85 years or so!

It was very evident to Wesley that animals know, understand, and think about many things. This was so obvious to him that he made very few efforts to illustrate or validate it. He defined "understanding" as "a capacity of apprehending whatever objects were brought before it, and of judging concerning them."[13] Thus understood, "the barrier between men and brutes" is "not reason. Set aside that ambiguous term and exchange it for the plain word, understanding, and who can deny that brutes have this? We may as well deny that they have sight or hearing."[14]

To elaborate a bit, anyone who has spent much time around animals (as Wesley did with his horses) knows that they are smart. In fact, they often "outsmart" us! They know many things. They can figure things out. They can solve problems with their own minds or consciousness. Within limits more severe than our own, they can anticipate the future. Even without language they can somehow envision future details, represent future possibilities to themselves, assess the desirability or undesirability of various outcomes, and freely choose between or among them. We know from our experience with them that they have decided preferences, likes, and dislikes. Beyond that, they can devise and execute clever strategies for achieving their goals and for avoiding undesirable consequences. Clearly, by degrees, non-human animals are rational animals, and if rationality is one aspect of the image of God, they also have it. If knowledge is the image of God in us, it is also present in them.

Human beings have many desirable capabilities in addition to reason and knowledge, but what? And do the animals also have them? Animals have *will* as well as reason and knowledge. This means that they have real feelings, desires, emotions, affections, moods, and attitudes. They are sentient beings capable of experiencing pleasures and pains. They enjoy life, as we do, and they suffer, as we do. They experience both "physical" or localized bodily pains and pleasures as well as "mental" or psychological pleasures, pains, feelings, desires, emotions, affections, moods, and attitudes. When the animals were created, Wesley said, "They had also a *will*, including various passions [affections or feelings], which likewise they still enjoy."[15] Wesley understood and explicitly rejected Descartes' view that animals are mere machines with no souls, minds, or consciousness. Descartes claimed that nothing is going on inside of animals. They have no souls. Wesley was convinced that like us, non-human animals are conscious subjects or souls with real thoughts, desires, feelings, volitions, and experiences.

In addition to will—feelings, emotions, and desires—Wesley was convinced that animals have "*liberty*, a power of choice, a degree of which is still found in every creature."[16] We might call it "free will," though Wesley preferred "liberty." Degrees of liberty, creativity, spontaneity, free will, originality, and self-determination pervade the universe and probably go much deeper into the natural order of things than Wesley ever imagined.

2. Non-human animals are even endowed with anticipations of morality. Wesley did not attribute the "moral image" of God to animals because he thought that they are "not moral agents," that is, they are not sufficiently knowledgeable to have, conform to, and violate moral rules or laws. He did indicate, however, that they exemplify a "shadowy resemblance" of a few genuine *moral virtues*, specifically, obedience, gratitude, reverence for proper authorities, and benevolence. As he described their original state in Eden, (with significant traces lingering thereafter),

> And as a loving obedience to God was the perfection of men, so a loving obedience to man was the perfection of brutes. And as long as they continued in this they were happy after their kind; happy in the right state and the right use of their respective faculties. Yea, and so long they had some shadowy resemblance of even *moral goodness*. For they had gratitude to man for benefits received, and a reverence for him. They had likewise a kind of benevolence to each other, unmixed with any contrary temper.[17]

All animals were originally like the ones we identify as "domesticated" or "tame," Wesley thought. None were wild or predatory. Wildness, death, predation, and pain all resulted from Adam's sin, (a view to which we can no longer subscribe). The important thing is that some moral virtues were and are there by degrees in non-human animals. Even benevolence is there, but usually only to members of their own clan or species. In that respect, they are not much different from us!

We know today that many animals are very loving and devoted parents. They work hard to care for and nurture their young, and they get great soul-fulfilment, satisfaction, and enjoyment from this. They make great personal sacrifices for them, care deeply about them and act accordingly, and they grieve for their loss. They care for and cooperate with their kin and close associates. Some animals don't do these things very well, but some people don't either! Precedents for and anticipations of human morality in the animal world are now being seriously studied, particularly in other primates like bonobos, chimpanzees, orangutans, and gorillas. We have learned that without language they understand, socially enforce, obey, and sometimes violate simple moral rules designed for mutual well-being. Their primitive morality usually applies only within their own clan, kin, or species, *as does ours* in our "natural state." Within limits, some primates learn to speak with their hands and communicate using our sign language for the deaf. They do not have vocal cords suitable for speech as we know it.

3. Animals too are loved by God, who is greatly concerned for their happiness and welfare. God understands the pains and losses that animals inflict on one another and that we maliciously inflict upon them. God "knoweth all their pain,"[18] but "as 'the Lord is loving to every man', so 'his mercy is over all his works' [Psalms 145:16]—all that have sense, all that are capable of pleasure or pain, of happiness or misery."[19] Animals too are "the offspring of one common Father, the creatures of the same God of love," and at the end of time as we know it, God will deliver them from "The horrid state of things which at present obtains."[20]

God positively values each and every animal and is concerned for their individual happiness and well-being, but God does not value them as much as human beings, Wesley thought. God recognizes, as we should, that for all of their image of God qualities, including elemental reason and benevolence, we have at least one important ability that they do not have, and this alone would give us more value than the animals. What is it? "But it is this: man is capable of God; the inferior creatures are not. We have no ground to believe that they are in any degree capable of knowing, loving, or obeying God." "Being capable of God" thus means: knowing, loving, and obeying God. "This is the specific difference between man and brute—the great gulf which they cannot pass over."[21] Thus, Wesley thought, we are more valuable than non-human animals, because *in kind* we at least have this one "good-making" capacity that they do not have. Maybe even here we should be cautious and not too overconfident!

Also, *in degree* we excel non-human animals in *all* of the image of God qualities that we share. Said Wesley, "God regards everything that he hath made in its own order, and in proportion to that measure of his own image which he had stamped upon it."[22] In other words, God values and ranks everything in proportion to its actual worth—measured ultimately against God's own worth. For this reason, "the Father of all has a tender regard for his lowest creatures, and . . . in consequence of this he will make them large amends for all they suffer while under their present bondage, yet I dare not affirm that he has an *equal regard* for them and for the children of men. . . . [God] regards man much more."[23] Presumably, so should we. None of our differences from animals justify our cruelty toward, injustices to, or mistreatments of them.

4. Animals, like people, should be treated by us in harmony with God's own mercy and compassion, guided by the Golden Rule. Wesley did not work out many details regarding our ethical relations with and treatments of animals, but he clearly thought that God "directs us to be tender of even the meaner creatures, to show mercy to these also."[24] Indeed, we should apply the Golden Rule to our moral relations with both animals and human beings. We ought to teach this to our children at a very early age. Christian parents should not allow their children

> to hurt or give pain to anything that has life. They will not permit them to rob birds' nests, much less to kill anything without necessity; not even snakes, which are as innocent as worms, or toads, which, notwithstanding their ugliness, and the ill name they lie under, have been proved over and over to be as harmless as flies. Let them extend in its measure the rule of doing as they would be done by, to every animal whatsoever.[25]

Wesley's brief discussion of our ethical relations with animals still leaves us with many unsolved problems about how to apply the Golden Rule to current issues like factory farming, commercial and medical experimentation on animals, vegetarianism, and the unhealthiness and ill environmental effects of eating meat. Wesley was an off-and-on vegetarian, mostly on, but mainly for self-interested reasons, that is, primarily for its personal health benefits. The extent to which he practiced vegetarianism for *moral* reasons like treating animals as we would wish to be treated if we were in their place, is unclear. Yet, what he did say about our concerns for and duties toward animals is highly relevant to present-day ethics and animals concerns and discussions. Once again, he got us off to a really good start.

A few current websites attribute the following quote to Wesley: "I believe in my heart that faith in Jesus Christ can and will lead us beyond an exclusive concern for the well-being of other human beings to a broader concern for the well-being of the birds in our backyards, the fish in our rivers, and every living creature on the face of the earth." We may wish that Wesley had written these words, but this is actually a bogus quote. No website ever cites its original source or location in Wesley writings. This quote is Wesleyan in spirit, but attributing it directly to Wesley himself is unethical.

Wesley really did insist very clearly that not being aware of the sacredness of animals and of "anything that has life" and of everything that exists at all, is a kind of "practical atheism." His authentic words about this profoundly affirm what we would call "creation care."

> God is in all things, and that we are to see the Creator in the glass of every creature; that we should use and look upon nothing as separate from God, which indeed is a kind of practical Atheism; but, with a true magnificence of thought, survey heaven and earth, and all that is therein, as contained by God in the hollow of His hand, who by His intimate presence holds them all in being, who pervades and actuates the whole created frame, and is, in a true sense, the soul of the universe.[26]

5. and 6. Astonishing to most of us, Wesley affirmed that animals too have *immortal souls* or spirits, and they too are *going to Heaven* in a re-embodied state. More precisely, they will be present body and soul in the

final "New Creation." The final state of things that Wesley expected to "come to pass when this world is no more,"[27] will be a "New Creation."[28] "Heaven," as we might call it, will actually be a newly created universe free from all of the imperfections of this one. In the final New Creation, there will be no more evils of any kind, no more diseases, natural disasters, killings, deaths, pains, suffering, sorrows, strife, sins, or conflicts of any description. All re-embodied or resurrected person and animals will live in harmony, peace, and happiness in the presence of one another and of God, Wesley thought. The New Creation will be a highly social world, not a solitary beatific vision.

All the non-human animals who ever lived will be present in the New Creation—re-embodied, resurrected, restored, enriched, and elevated. All will live together in a peaceable kingdom. There will be no war any more and no more predators. "[T]he lion shall eat straw like the ox. . . . They shall not hurt or destroy in all my holy mountain" [Isaiah 11:7, 9].[29] Animals will be fully compensated for all the evils they suffered in this world, especially at our hands. Our own human capabilities will be elevated to where the angels are now, and the animals will be elevated to where we are now.[30] So Wesley supposed. He expected to be reunited with all of his faithful horses in the world to come.

No matter what reservations we might have about all of this, we must concede that this is an incredibly appealing "eschatological" vision. Obviously, such a newly created universe would have to be very large to accommodate all the people and animals who ever lived, but, as some philosophers suggest, in a hotel with an infinite number of rooms, there will always be room for one more. Expressed theologically, and in Wesley's spirit, we could say that there is always room in God's infinite love for at least one more—animal or human.

About the reality of this forthcoming New Creation, we will just have to wait and see. The task God has given to us at present is to live the most meaningful, loving, helpful, harmonious, fulfilled, happy, abundant, and Godlike lives we can—with one another, with the animals, and with all of God's creation. We should be grateful for what we are and have right now. Everything else is in God's hands. We can only trust that God will know and do what is best.

Notes

1. Anton C. Pegis, ed., *Basic Writings of Saint Thomas Aquinas*, New York: Random House, 1945, 1, 21.
2. Wesley, "On Divine Providence," *Works*, 2, 540-541. Italics added. See also Wesley, "On the Fall of Man," *Works*, 2, 409, and Wesley, "The General Deliverance," *Works*, 2, 438-439. In some of these, Wesley includes a capacity for "self-motion" as an additional natural image of God property.
3. Wesley, "On the Fall of Man," *Works*, 2, 409.
4. Ibid.
5. Wesley, "The End of Christ's Coming," *Works*, 2, 474.
6. Ibid.
7. Wesley, "The New Birth," *Works*, 2, 188. On the image as love, see also Wesley, "The Righteousness of Faith," *Works*, 1, 205 and Wesley, "The One Thing Needful," *Works*, 4, 355.
8. Wesley, "The End of Christ's Coming," *Works*, 2, 475.
9. Wesley, "The New Birth," *Works*, 2, 188.
10. Wesley, "The End of Christ's Coming," *Works*, 2, 475-476.
11. Wesley, "The General Deliverance," *Works*, 2, 440-441.
12. Ibid., 438.
13. Ibid., 439.
14. Ibid., 441.
15. Ibid., 440.
16. Ibid., 440-441.
17. Ibid., 441.
18. Ibid., 445.
19. Ibid., 437.
20. Wesley, "The New Creation," *Works*, 2, 509.
21. Wesley, "The General Deliverance," *Works*, 2, 441.
22. Ibid., 448.
23. Ibid., 447.
24. Ibid., 437.
25. Wesley, "The Almost Christian," *Works*, 1, 141; "Catholic Spirit," *Works*, 2, 89; "On the Education of Children," *Works*, 3, 360.
26. Wesley, "Upon Our Lord's Sermon on the Mount, III," *Works*, 1, 516-517.

27. Wesley, "The New Creation," *Works*, 2, 502.
28. Ibid., 500-510.
29. Wesley, "The General Deliverance," *Works*, 2, 446.
30. Ibid., 446, 448.

Chapter 8

The Goodness of God

What is God like? Why is God supremely worshipful? Why does God *deserve* to be loved with all our hearts, souls, minds, and strength? Wesley had an answer. Citing Psalm 100:5, it is because "God is Good:"[1] "For the Lord is Good; his mercy is everlasting; and his truth endureth to all generations." Because God is good, God deserves to be called "our Father." Indeed, God is supremely good, perfect, unsurpassable, and this is why God is supremely worshipful and entitled to our total devotion, love, and service. God has or is everything that any being ought to have or be in order to count as supremely good, perfect, and worshipful. God's perfect-making characteristics are traditionally called "attributes." Only a few of God's attributes as discussed by Wesley will be considered here—God's power, love, and presence—but keep in mind, "The nature of God.... necessarily includes all good."[2] So what you will get here isn't the whole story! God exists as the greatest conceivable goodness. That is why God deserves our complete devotion.

Christians and others who affirm God's reality do not always agree about what God is like. They may disagree about what God's "attributes" mean even when they verbally agree about what they are and that God has them. Human value judgments inevitably influence how we understand God's goodness, perfections, and desirable qualities or attributes. "God" is both a value concept and a reality concept. In the end, you will just have to decide for yourself about what God is like, and what God would have to be like to be truly "good." But try to do so in an enlightened, reflective, informed, unbiased, and unpressured manner. Wesley did, and his thoughts about God can enlighten us.

Philosophically, Wesley thought, we discern God's attributes or perfections by first identifying what we value within ourselves, and then we assign those desirable qualities to God. "This we do in the best manner we can," he wrote, "by removing from him all the imperfections of the creatures, and attributing to him all their perfections, especially those of our own minds."[3] None of God's attributes can be understood literally, only analogically, he claimed, because all such words apply infinitely to God but only finitely to us.[4] So much for theological literalism!

God's Power

Most of us would agree that God has to be immensely powerful to deserve our total service, devotion, and awe, but just how powerful is that? We say that God is Sovereign, Almighty, Omnipotent, but just how powerful is that? Well, God has enough power to create whole universes out of nothing, and that is a lot of power! But does having this much power mean that God absolutely controls and causes everything that happens within the universe?

On the surface, "omnipotent" literally suggests "all power," but does this mean both *having* and *using* all the power that there is? Is God the absolute cause of everything that happens all the time and everywhere, including every choice that we make, good or bad? Does God both *have* and *exercise* all the power that there is, or does God graciously *share* some of his power with his creatures? Does absolutely everything come from the exercise of *God's* power, or do some things follow from *our* creative exercise of our own inherent powers? Is God an Absolute Sovereign who can and does do anything he pleases with impunity simply because he has the power to do it? Some of the biggest disagreements in theology are over how to answer these questions.

How should we proceed to answer such questions? We must further ask, What would be the very best, the most worshipful, the most desirable, the most perfect kind of divine power? What kind of power must God have in order to be *Good*? Even here there is plenty of room for honest disagreement.

Christians honestly disagree about the correct answer to our questions about God's power. We may be puzzled ourselves. It all depends on what we judge to be *the most desirable kind* of divine power. What kind of power must God have and exercise in order to be supremely good? Fundamental spiritual and moral values are at stake here. Such norms come sharply into focus over the doctrine of predestination.

St. Paul taught predestination in the 8th and 9th chapters of Romans, and St. Augustine (354-430 CE) forcefully championed and established it as Christian orthodoxy. Almost everyone after Augustine and before Wesley affirmed predestination except for a very small handful of heretics like Pelagius (360-418) and Jacob Arminius (1560-1609). John Wesley sided with the heretics, with Arminius in particular. Why? Before considering his answer, let's first try to understand what predestination really means and what the Bible says about it.

Many people think that predestination determines only who goes to Heaven and who goes to Hell, but it actually covers a whole lot more than that. It includes absolutely everything that ever happens, from the existence and motion of every electron and atom, to the fate and decisions of every society, nation, and individual. Everything, good or bad, that ever occurs expresses God's predestined "plan" or "will." Everything is brought into being by God's all-inclusive, all-controlling causation or power. God as Absolute Sovereign *has* all power at his disposal, *uses* it, and does not share it with others. God plans, wills, and causes absolutely everything. So says predestination.

The trouble is, if God originates and causes *everything*, this includes every existing moral atrocity and every horrible natural catastrophe. We originate nothing; we effectively cause nothing. God is purely active; we are totally passive. We merely carry out the agenda that God planned for us and programmed into us from eternity. From eternity, God predetermined every choice that we ever make in time and history. If we make bad decisions, we will go to Hell; if we make good decisions, we will go to Heaven; *but* God causes all of our dispositions, desires, and decisions to be exactly as they are. We do *make* decisions, for better or for worse, but we do not *originate* them. God alone does. God is the sole originative or creative causal agent in the universe, and beyond.

Predestination usually goes along with another doctrine—the small "saving remnant." Protestant thinkers like Luther and Calvin insisted that God predestines "the great bulk of mankind" to Hell. Only a very few people, only a small saving remnant, the elect, are predestined for Heaven. St. Paul said in Romans 9:27, following Isaiah 10:22-23, that although the children of Israel are as plentiful "as the sand of the sea, only a remnant of them will be saved." This saving remnant is very small indeed, says Calvinism and all other Christian predestinationisms. Very few people are destined for Heaven. Why not? God consigns most people to Hell for utterly inscrutable reasons simply because he has the power to do so. God has mercy and compassion on whoever he will, and God arbitrarily hardens the hearts of whoever he will (Romans 9:15, 18). God has the authority to do this simply because God has or is absolute sovereign power. Predestinationists value absolute power far more than any of the rest of God's attributes. Nothing stands in its way, not even love, compassion, and justice. Do you agree? Wesley thought that God's goodness stands in its way.

Why did Wesley reject predestination? That God elected only a small saving remnant for Heaven may be taught in the Bible, Wesley recognized, but he rejected all parts and interpretations of the Bible that are "absurd." Predestination implies that God is unloving, unjust, morally reprehensible, and just plain mean, and what could be more absurd than that? In response to George Whitefield's scriptural view of predestination, Wesley declared, *"No scripture can mean that God is not love, or that his mercy is not over all his works."*[5]

Wesley insisted that biblical predestination is logically and morally incompatible with "God is love," the very heart of the Bible and true religion. He was convinced that God loves everybody everywhere and wills to save *all*, not just an arbitrarily chosen few. Most importantly, Christ died for *all*, not just an elect few.

Wesley was a Universalist, but he did not think that everyone will be saved. Some people, he thought, will freely refuse God's gifts of grace, mercy, and love. Predestination assumes that God loves only a tiny fragment of humanity, only an arbitrarily chosen few, the elect, the small saving remnant. Correspondingly, God absolutely hates the "great bulk of mankind." All sinners and their sins are "wholly defiled" and are "infinitely odious" to God, said Calvinistic Jonathan Edwards, and they deserve God's infinite hatred and infinite punishment. Of course, says predestination, from eternity God planned and caused them to be precisely the "odious" sinners that they are. God predetermines every sinful decision, then punishes sinners for making them. "Mercifully," Calvinists affirm, God arbitrarily loves and saves a few anyway. Wesley did not think that this was very merciful, loving, or just!

So, predestination severely limits the *scope or inclusiveness* of God's love. It is also incompatible with God's moral goodness, love, and justice in another way. Wesley thought that a *morally good*, loving, and just God just wouldn't do it! Love itself is at stake here. So is justice. Predestination is not compatible with moral goodness. It overvalues God's power (sovereignty) at the expense of God's goodness, love, mercy, and justice. Wesley explained, it "destroys all his [God's] attributes at once. It overturns his justice, mercy, and truth. Yea, it represents the most holy God as worse than the devil; as both more false, more cruel, and more unjust."[6] God's power, so understood, conflicts with God's holiness, love, justice, forgiveness, and moral goodness—given freely *to all*.

The most conscionable and consistent Christian view, Wesley proposed, is that "All his attributes are inseparably joined."[7] This means that they are in harmony with, and not in conflict with, one another. The God of Lutherans, Calvinists, and all predestinationists "is not the God of the Christians,"[8] Their God is worse than the devil! God's power must be understood in a way that makes it compatible with God's holiness, love, justice, righteousness, and worshipfulness.

There are many different and incompatible kinds of power: for example, the power to persuade versus the power to coerce. Some kinds of power are irreconcilable with other kinds, so God can't have and exercise *all kinds* of power all at once. God has at least one kind of power, Wesley thought, that the God of predestination does not have, namely, the power to give away some of his power. God does exactly this when he distributes liberty of choice throughout all of creation—most obviously to us and the animals. Having liberty of choice, or "free will" as many would say, means that we *originate* our own decisions. God does not originate them for us, or program them into us, especially not our moral and spiritual choices.

Wesley, the Universalist, held that God is "willing that all men should be saved, yet not willing to force them thereto;" God treats us "as reasonable creatures, endued with understanding to discern what is good, and liberty either to accept or refuse it."[9] God's graciousness toward all is resistible, not irresistible, as it is for the elect few according to Calvinism. Wesley explained that God would be "the only proper agent in the universe; unless so far as he imparts a spark of his active, self-determining nature to created spirits."[10] So, God gives away some of God's power to us. God is not the only creative agent in the universe. Our loving and self-limiting God gave us liberty of choice. By God's grace, we are co-agents, co-originators, co-creators, co-workers with God. We originate and are responsible for the free choices we make. We initiate our own decisions, not God, so we are responsible for them and for their good or bad consequences, not God.

Having all power, but not *using* it all, having it but generously and lovingly giving some of it away, is what harmonizes God's omnipotence with God's holiness, justice, mercy, love, and moral goodness. Morally and spiritually good and perfect power is the power to empower others, to share power, and this self-limiting power is very different from the power of absolute control.

It could be argued that God's sharing power was not a *voluntary* choice, not one that could have been otherwise, for a truly good and loving God. It would be a matter of divine *necessity* if, as Wesley said, God "necessarily includes all good."[11] Perhaps sharing power, self-limitation, *kenosis*, is a moral necessity of God's very nature. It is what supremely worshipful love and justice would do and could not avoid doing.

Wesley did not intend to create a new church, but the Methodist Church was the first Christian denomination of any consequence to reject predestination and affirm "free will" or "liberty of choice," as Wesley phrased it. We can and should take great pride in this today. Methodists believe in free will! Many other church groups now reject predestination, or have greatly soften up on it, thanks largely to Wesley's expanding influence.

God's Feelings, Love, and Compassion

Does God have any real feelings? Most ordinary Christians would say, "Yes, obviously, for God is love." We know that real feelings as well as real thoughts are present in *our own* love for God, other people, animals, ourselves, mind-less things, doctrines, or whatever we happen to love. Love by definition and by analogy involves feelings. Except for being infinite, God's love is no different from ours. Of course, that's a big difference! The deeper our love and compassion, the more intense and sustained are our feelings. How could this be otherwise with God?

Are you ready for another big surprise? This is not what most of the "big name" theologians who came before Wesley said! Most denied that God has any real feelings at all! God does not have any of the positive *affections* or feelings that constitute love, most said. God does not experience any of the *sufferings* involved in compassion. Compassion suffers with those who suffer, but God in himself doesn't have it. We may experience God as if he had compassion, but he doesn't. God absolutely does not suffer anything in any way, they said. God wouldn't be perfect if God suffers! So is suffering with those who suffer (compassion) a perfection or an imperfection?

Most ordinary Christians believe that God really is compassionate, but the Christian theologians who came along before Wesley declared that this is wrong. For centuries, the church branded as *heresy* the view that God has any real feelings about anything. This heresy has the technical name of "*patripassianism.*" This heresy says that "God the Father *does* have real passions or feelings," and that is why it is a heresy. Historically, Christian thinkers, catholic and protestant, condemned and rejected this belief. The official view was that *we experience God as if* he has real feelings of love and compassion, but *in himself,* there are no real feelings of any kind at all! Did your minister ever tell you that? Did you ever hear a Sunday morning sermon on that? If not, you might thank God and John Wesley!

To illustrate the extremity of the official traditional view, when theologians like Athanasius and Anselm asked if God suffered while Jesus agonized on the cross, their answer was emphatically, "No." Only the *human nature* of Jesus suffered on the cross. His *divine nature* felt absolutely nothing. God the Father was totally "impassible" (unfeeling) through it all. Does that make good sense to you? It didn't to Wesley.

Where did all the classical Christian thinkers get the idea that God has no feelings, that all feelings are imperfections, that all feelings are unworthy of God? From the Greek philosophers, not from the Bible. Philosophy can contribute very positively to competent theological reflection, but, to be honest about it, some philosophy is not helpful. Occasionally, but not always, we must ask, "What does Athens have to do with Jerusalem?" The synthesis of Greek philosophy with Biblical religion instigated by very early Jewish and Christian thinkers was both a blessing and a curse. The curse was that it greatly distorted many important biblical insights. The blessing was and is that rationality, accuuthfulness, clarity, comprehensiveness, and logic have important places in good theological thinking, as Wesley well understood.

The Greek philosophers, not the authors of the Bible, judged that all feelings are either too low in value or too inherently bad to be attributed to God. Aristotle, not the Bible, said that God is "impassible" and has no feelings at all. Aristotle's God does nothing but think about thinking and has no knowledge about or feelings for us or for anything else. Regrettably, before Wesley, most Catholic and Protestant thinkers agreed with Aristotle that God has no feelings.

Even the "First Article of Religion" of the Church of England declared, "There is but one living and true God, everlasting, without body, parts, or passions." When he sent them to Methodists in America after the Revolutionary War, Wesley scrapped fifteen of the thirty nine Anglican Articles of Religion, and he changed some of the others. So much for tradition! The American version of this particular Article omitted the "*without . . . passions*" phrase. Scholars are not sure that Wesley himself deleted it. Perhaps later American Methodists did. Clearly, though, Wesley believed that God is "*with passions.*" He thought that God has real feelings of love and compassion of infinite proportions.

Some very extreme Greek philosophers claimed that all feelings or passions are downright bad, thus altogether undesirable, both in God and in us. The Stoics went to this extreme. They taught that we should suppress all of our own feelings and live by reason alone—as if this were even possible. They would have rejected the Christian love commandments if they had known about them. They taught that we should never allow ourselves to love, be emotionally involved with, or get attached to anyone—not our friends, not our children, not our spouses, nor anyone else—lest we be hurt when something bad happens to them. The Stoics lacked the courage to love, with all its risks. They refused to identify themselves with or have real feelings for anything or anyone. Their view was that all feelings are bad or undesirable in both us and God. Suppressing all of our own feelings and living by reason alone would be the godlike thing for us to do. Do you agree? Wesley did not.

Common sense says, and most ordinary Christians believe, that *some* of our human feelings like hatred, anger, envy, and vengeance are undesirable, but *others* like love, mercy, compassion, forgiveness, and a keen sense of justice are very good and highly desirable. Yet, the view of classical Christian thinkers before Wesley was that *divine* goodness excludes *all* feelings, *all* passions, both desirable and undesirable, because no feelings could be good or desirable in God. Feelings were imperfections, not perfections.

In Wesley's very different view, a God without feelings just would not be good or perfect; God's perfection in love and compassion must include all such feelings. Wesley decisively opposed the dominant tradition. His writings frequently affirm God's real feelings of love, mercy, and compassion. This is most obvious, perhaps, where he attributed "will" to God. Given his definition of it, "will" consists of feelings (passions), desires, emotions, affections, moods, approvals, etc. The "religious affections" belong as much to God as to us. Of course, God has only desirable feelings, but they are very real. Wesley wrote, "For he [God] created man in his own image: a spirit like himself; a spirit endued with understanding, with will or *affections*, and liberty."[12] John agreed with his brother Charles that God, as represented by Jesus, is "all compassion, pure unbounded love." The Wesleys really meant it! There was no double-talk in their affirmation of God's love and compassion.

Methodists today make a very large and positive place for feelings, emotions, and affections in true religion and morality. Some Wesleyans have been accused of going overboard with this! We are created in the image of God as love, Wesley affirmed, and love is primarily a matter of the heart, not of the head. "Heart" was Wesley's non-literal metaphor for the affective or feeling parts of our souls. God also has a heart, again speaking non-literally, and love and compassion are the essence of it. "Thou, O man of God, stand fast in love, in the image of God wherein thou art made. If thou will remain in life, keep the commandments which are now written in thy heart. Love the Lord thy God with all thy heart. Love as thyself every soul that He hath made."[13]

Loving both God and any or all of God's creatures involves identifying with them so intensely that our differences from them no longer matter. God loves that way, and maybe we should. Our differences are very real, but what happens to others, whether good or bad, is experienced as happening to us—if we truly love them. Love involves profound psychological, evaluational, and emotional or affective union with those loved. In love, two become one, while remaining two. When we intensely love another, whether Divine or human, that other becomes an integral part of our own personal self-identity. Union with God is union in love. So is union with our "neighbor."

God's Presence

Omnipresence is one of God's traditional attributes. Wesley emphasized and explained it. So what does God's "omnipresence" mean, and what practical or spiritual difference does it make?

If your child or grandchild asks you, "Where is God?" how would you answer? You might say, "God is in heaven," but that answer would be a very incomplete. You might say, "God is everywhere," and that would be a better answer, the right answer. But what exactly does this mean in theory and in practice?

Wesley insisted that God is a spirit without a body; yet God is present everywhere. Do these claims conflict? To resolve such tensions, today's process thinkers suggest that any created universe would be God's body, and God is the soul of that body. Both we and God, they suggest, are embodied souls. Wesley himself said more than once that God is the "soul of the universe," but he did not take the next obvious step and say that the universe is God's body. Process theologians do. Human souls are best understood as fields of psycho-physical energy that pervade our own brains and bodies. God's presence includes and permeates all of reality. Acts, 17:28 says that God is that supreme reality within whom we live and move and have our being. Wesley often cited this verse with approval.[14]

Wesley connected God's omniscience (knowing everything) with God's omnipresence (being everywhere). To know (and influence but not determine) everything that happens everywhere, God would have to be present everywhere and everywhen.[15] Said Wesley, "There is no point of space, whether within or without the bounds of creation, where God is not," and "The universal God dwelleth in universal space."[16] He did not say explicitly that the world or universe is the body of God, but he came very close to it. He did say very clearly that God is the soul of the world. In his words, "The soul is a spirit, an intelligent, immortal spirit, an active spirit, herein resembling God, the Father of spirits, and the soul of the world."[17]

If the universe is the body of God, how should we revere, respect, and treat God's body—our environment, our own critical life-support system? Even if we don't use the "body" metaphor, we can still wonder how we should revere, respect, and treat everything if God is truly present everywhere. God's omnipresence has great theoretical, spiritual, moral, and practical significance. Even if we believe "with the top of our heads" that God is everywhere, we may not believe this "with the bottom of our hearts." God is everywhere, but most of the time we are only dimly aware of this. Regrettably, God's universal presence seems to make very little practical difference to the moral or spiritual quality of our lives or our behaviors. Most of the time, we just don't think about it, and we just don't care. We can *do* better and *be* better. Wesley can help us.

Wesley thought that we have "spiritual senses" in addition to our five "external senses" of sight, hearing, smell, taste, and touch. Our spiritual senses give us a direct experiential or "experimental" awareness of the presence of God in us and in all other things.[18] Sadly, these inner spiritual senses usually do not work very well for us. Our sinfulness and our low spiritual and moral development prevent both our spiritual senses and our consciences from working properly. Wesley explained,

> So it is with him that is born of God. Before that great change is wrought, although he subsists by him, in whom all that have life 'live, and move, and have their being', yet he is not sensible of God; he does not feel, he has no inward consciousness of His presence. He does not perceive that divine breath of life, without which he cannot subsist a moment. Nor is he sensible of any of the things of God. They make no impression upon his soul. God is continually calling to him from high, but he heareth not; his ears are shut; so that the 'voice of the charmer' is lost to him, 'charm he never so wisely'. He seeth not the things of the Spirit of God, the eyes of his understanding being closed, and utter darkness covering his whole soul, surrounding him on every side. It is true he may have some faint dawnings of life, some small beginnings of spiritual motion; but as yet he has no spiritual senses capable of discerning spiritual objects. Consequently, he 'discerneth not the things of the Spirit of God; he cannot know them, because they are spiritually discerned.'[19]

After their spiritual senses are awakened and begin to function, saintly souls begin to experience something immensely important, something that lost souls largely lack. Sanctification, the process of spiritual growth, involves an awakened sensitivity to the *universal* presence of God in ourselves, in all others, in all things, and to God's *particular* presence in special people, happenings, times, things, and places. Do our ministers and churches help us to grow in such ways? Are they fully engaged in the formation of souls in their care, with God's help? Do they help us to find God everywhere? Our developed spiritual senses make us aware of the sacredness of all events, inanimate things, living things, animals, people, and of God himself, in whom we live and move and have our being. This greatly affects the quality and abundance of our own daily lives. With our whole hearts or whole persons, we come to revere and respect all of creation, along with its Creator. We become more and more aware of God as all in all. We also find God as specially present in particular happenings, persons, times, and places. The "veil" that hides God lifts.

Spiritual growth affects the seriousness, intensity, constancy, and practice of our sense of the presence of God everywhere and at all times. Amazingly, spiritually developed persons (real saints) actually value the mind-less things of the world even more than worldly people do, for they experience even inanimate things as holy and pervaded by God. They realize that everything is infused with the reality and presence of God. God is even present in evil, not as willing or causing it, but as being compassionately affected by it and immensely hurt by it. Saintly persons keenly sense that "every creature is God's and he is everywhere present, in all, and over all. He is as intimately present in earth as in heaven."[20] Every human body, every human act, every physical or material object and process, and all of the very smallest details of existence become sacred. "One branch of the worshipping God in spirit and in truth," Wesley wrote, "is the *keeping* his outward commandments. To glorify him, therefore *with our bodies as well as with our spirits*, to go through *outward work with hearts* lifted up to him, to make our *daily employment* a sacrifice to God, *to buy and sell, to eat and drink, to his glory*: this is worshipping *God* in spirit and in truth as much as the praying to him in a wilderness."[21] So, do you constantly buy and sell, eat and drink, to God's glory?

Exactly how our increased religious affections and sensitivity to the presence of God should be expressed externally in devotional Acts of Piety has been a matter of considerable controversy among Wesleyans. Perhaps Pentecostal Wesleyans have been the most emotionally and overtly expressive. Mainline Methodists are usually a bit more reserved. Wesley repeatedly warned against what was called "enthusiasm," in his day. This was then understood to be *excessive* emotionalism and professing special divine inspirations without rational or scriptural constraints. Yet, despite all the pitfalls, our religious affections and sensitivities have a very legitimate place in our services of worship and deeds of mercy. We should have Godlike love and compassion for all; and we should "see" God in all.

Consider how Wesley described increased sensitivity to the presence of God everywhere and at all times.

> They [the pure in heart] now see him by faith (the veil of flesh being made, as it were, transparent), even in these his lowest works, in all that surrounds them, in all that God has created and made. They see him in the height above, and in the depth beneath; they see him filling all in all. The pure in heart see all things full of God. They see him in the firmament of heaven; in the moon, walking in brightness; in the sun, when he rejoiceth as a giant to run his course. They see him 'making the clouds his chariots, and walking upon the wings of the wind.' They see him 'preparing rain for the earth', 'and blessing the increase of it'; 'giving grass for the cattle, and green herb for the use of man'. They see the Creator of all wisely governing all, and 'upholding all things by the word of his power'. 'O Lord, our Governor, how excellent is Thy name in all the world!'[22]

God, Wesley thought, is that all-inclusive and omnipresent reality who "fills heaven and earth" (Jeremiah 23:24) and "in whom we live and move and have our being" (Acts 17:28). Although God includes all, God still allows created spirits some degree of independence, freedom, self-creativity, and personal room for spiritual and moral growth (sanctification). This includes increasing sensitivity to his universal presence. "God acts everywhere, and therefore is everywhere; . . . God acts in heaven, in earth, and under the earth, throughout the whole compass of creation . . . strongly and sweetly influencing all, and yet without destroying the liberty of his rational creatures."[23] Today, such a worldview is called "panentheism" or "process theism." There are differences,[24] but Wesley definitely anticipated it. God includes all but does not determine all. God is passive when we make our own decisions, active when he makes his own, but present everywhere one way or the other. We act upon God; God acts upon us. The use or exercise of power isn't all one-sided. The power to give some power away is perfect power.

The general presence of God in all things still allows for the particular presence of God in special sacred happenings, persons, places, times, and individuals. God particular presence with and in us here and now is what Wesley called the Holy Spirit. God as Spirit is the all-embracing reality, active and present everywhere, including here and now. When we are spiritually awakened and fully mature, the Holy Spirit testifies to our individual spirits that we in particular are accepted, forgiven, reconciled, restored, and loved as "Sons" of God. (Daughters, too!) Those with lesser degrees of spiritual maturity (mere "Servants," Wesley suggested) rarely if ever experience this.[25] The Holy Spirit was in and with the saints of the Bible, the ages, all nations, and of today. That Divine Spirit is affected by and suffers because of and with all who sin and suffer. The Spirit also comforts and encourages all who mourn, all who rejoice, all who do the works of love, and all who need to rest.

So, how sensitive are you to the presence of God—all in all, and within you?

Notes

1. Wesley, "Upon Our Lord's Sermon on the Mount," *Works*, 1, 578.

2. Wesley, "Original Sin," *Works*, 2, 175.

3. Wesley, *A Survey of the Wisdom of God in the Creation: A Compendium of Natural Philosophy*, 2, 433.

4. Ibid., and 443-444.

5. Wesley, "Free Grace," *Works*, 3, 556. Italics added.

6. Ibid., 3, 556.

7. Wesley, "Predestination Calmly Considered," Outler, 435.

8. Ibid., 451.

9. Ibid., 450.

10. John Wesley, "A Thought on Necessity," *The Works of the Reverend John Wesley, A.M.*, ed. John Emory. (New York: The Methodist Episcopal Church, 1831), 6, 214.

11. Wesley, "Original Sin," *Works*, 2, 175.

12. Wesley, "On Divine Providence," *Works*, 2, 540-541. Italics added.

13. Wesley, "The Righteousness of Faith," *Works*, 1, 205.

14. See *Works*, 4, 671 for references in Wesley's sermons.

15. Wesley, "On the Omnipresence of God," *Works*, 4, 41-44.

16. Ibid., 42.

17. Wesley, "On the Fall of Man," *Works*, 2, 409.

18. A great deal more can be said about the spiritual senses and the omnipresence of God than is said here. For a much more detailed discussion see Edwards, *John Wesley's Values—and Ours*, 208-241,

19. Wesley, "The Great Privilege of Those that are Born of God," *Works*, 1, 433-434.

20. Wesley, "Upon Our Lord's Sermon on the Mount, III, *Works*, 1, 515.

21. Wesley, "Upon Our Lord's Sermon on the Mount, IV," *Works*, 1, 544. (Italics added.)

22. Ibid., 513-514. See also Wesley, "The Great Privilege of Those that are Born of God," *Works*, 1, 434-435.

23. Wesley, "On the Omnipresence of God," *Works*, 4, 42-43.

24. The main difference is that Wesley still subscribed to the classical view of God's "eternity" as consisting of a changeless "all time all at once," whereas process thinkers regard "eternity" as "everlasting" but constantly changing as God responds in real time to real people and happenings in history and nature. However, many things that Wesley said about God and the world are incompatible with his classical understanding of "eternity" and would make much better sense within a process understanding of eternity as everlasting but never finished.

25. Wesley, "On the Discoveries of Faith," *Works*, 4, 35-36.

Chapter 9

Means and Ends

Some good things are better than others. Wesley taught that we, like God, should love and value every good thing in proportion to its actual worth. To do this, we must at least understand the difference between means and ends and their respective kinds of worth. Means to ends are valuable because they are useful. They are instrumental or extrinsic goods. Ends are the goals to be reached by using proper means. Some ends are, in turn, means to other ends. Some are final ends, intrinsic goods. Wesley wrote, "Wisdom is the faculty of discerning the best ends, and the fittest means of attaining them,"[1] and "We should not expect the end without the means."[2]

Success in daily living depends partly on luck, partly on grace. It also depends on wisely choosing the best or most effective means to our goals or ends, and to selecting the best or most desirable ends. For example, we would like to know and choose the best way to educate ourselves and our children, the best way to win and please our lovers, the best way to earn a living, the best way to prepare for the future, the best way to serve God, the best way to love and help our neighbors, the best way to love and take care of ourselves. To be successful at anything, we must learn what is likely to cause what in the world, and what the results of our own personal actions are likely to be. And we must act accordingly. We must make well informed decisions.

Some courses of action are more likely to be successful than others. Some physical objects and personal actions better serve our purposes than others. Some human purposes or objectives are much better or more desirable than others. Wisdom recognizes that mind-less physical objects, and our own practical or bodily activities, are desirable as means to ends beyond themselves. Practical wisdom chooses the "fittest means" to our goals, as well as the very best goals, just as Wesley said.

Unwisely, we often choose ineffective means to our ends, or we choose undesirable and unworthy ends. In our ignorance and sinfulness, we often make very bad choices. If we are wise, we choose effective or "fit" means to our ends—the ones that are likely to get the job done, to take us where we really need to go, and to accomplish what we really want to accomplish. Wisdom will select the best practical, moral, and spiritual ends, as well as the best or most effective means to them. Having the ability to do this requires a lot of knowledge, education, practical training, and moral and spiritual development. Our ministers and church staffs, and our communion with other "saints" (church members and other spiritual examples or role models) should help us grow in such graces. So should our families, our friends, our schools, and our society. Corrupt societies make for corrupt people.

Confusing Means and Ends

Ignorance and sinfulness affect and infect the practical choices that we make. Often we confuse means with ends. We may mistakenly value useful means more than we value final ends. As Wesley indicated, our ignorance and sinfulness may cause us to value or love the mindless material "things of the world" for their own sake—as if they were the final ends, purposes, or goals of life. Their proper value, however, is in their usefulness as means for acquiring and sharing the basic necessities of life—and maybe even a few comforts. They may also be useful in serving and achieving some of our spiritual and moral ends. We value material resources correctly when we use them to benefit ourselves or others, but not when we see them as the final ends of life. Christian lives have higher purposes. The real value of money or wealth is in the human (or animal, or environmental) benefits to be expected from it. Money is a means for achieving other goals beyond money itself, preferably good goals, not sinful goals. Some people mistakenly love money for its own sake, as Jesus recognized.

Yes, some people habitually value the mind-less "things of the world" as if they were the final ends or goals of life. Theologians call such people "worldly." The disposition to wrongfully overvalue the material things of the world is "worldliness." The priorities of worldly people are really messed up. They value mind-less means as if they were final ends of life, and they undervalue, exploit, and abuse mind-full people and animals as if they were nothing more than means to their own personal selfish and short-sighted materialistic goals. We often call them "materialists." Most of us know real people like that.

In modern psychological terms, worldly people are only "half-brained." That is, they normally use only half of their brains, the left half where sensory perceptions, sensory words, and language itself are situated. They have very little holistic (whole-istic) grasp of desirable realities beyond sensory objects. They do not understand or experience what is really good or worthwhile for its own sake. Their right-brained capacities for inclusiveness, feelings, love, empathy, and intrinsic evaluation are not adequately very well developed, so they just do not use them.

Worldly people exploit, manipulate, deceive, suppress, and even enslave other people as a means to increasing their own property, possessions, profits, and social status. They treat final ends as mere means—and mere means as final ends. By nature (or because of early life experiences), they are psychologically oriented externally, not internally, and their primary value-objects are external, physical, and sensory. They have little right-brained holistic self-awareness or God-awareness—what spiritual thinkers call "inwardness." Many theologians say that worldliness is the most "natural," prevalent, and enduring sinful disposition or condition of human souls. Worldliness is the dominant feature of "original sin" or our "natural state." Of course, by God's prevenient grace, no real people are absolutely worldly. Worldliness is always a matter of degree, as is saintliness. But in some people, it is dominant.

Worldliness, Wesley said, involves "loving the world; desiring it for its own sake."[3] To worldly sinners, he said, "Thy affections are alienated from God, and scattered abroad over all the earth. All thy passions, both thy desires and aversions, thy joys and sorrows, thy hopes and fears, are out of frame, are either undue in their degree, or placed on *undue objects*."[4] That is their main problem; they overvalue "undue objects."

Worldliness is one kind of idolatry. It is a false religion, the religion of the everyday world. Worldly people are ultimately concerned with mindless sensory realities, not with God or people. Yet, they have a pervasive sense of meaninglessness. They are indeed devoted to "undue objects;" and their affections are "out of frame." Their pursuit of happiness does not yield real happiness. Their pleasures are only worldly pleasures.

They love and enjoy material or sensory things, but they have not yet learned to delight in spirits, souls, people, and God. Consider how Wesley described the "natural state" of worldly sinners:

> I mean love of the world, which is now as natural to every man as to love his own will. What is more natural to us than to seek happiness in the creature instead of the Creator? What more natural than the desire of the flesh? That is, of the pleasure of sense in every kind? . . . Sensual appetites, even those of the lowest kind, have, more or less, the dominion over him. They lead him captive, they drag him to and fro, in spite of his boasted reason. The man, with all his good breeding and other accomplishments, has no pre-eminence over the goat. Nay, it is much to be doubted whether the beast has not pre-eminence over him![5]

> We think of what we love; but we do not love God; therefore, we think not of him. Or if we are now and then constrained to think of him for a time . . . we drive [such thoughts] out as soon as we can, and return to what we love to think of. So that the world, and the things of the world—what we shall eat, what we shall drink, what we shall put on; what we shall see, what we shall hear, what we shall gain; how we shall please our senses or our imagination—takes up all our time, and engrosses all our thoughts. So long, therefore as we love the world, that is so long as we are in our natural state, all our thoughts, from morning to evening, and from evening to morning, are no other than wandering thoughts."[6]

> This is the sum of worldly happiness–to dress, and visit, and talk, and eat, and drink, and rise up to play.[7]

Don't get the wrong idea. Wesley did not regard the external sensory or physical world as evil. He regarded it as very good, but it should not be overvalued or exclusively valued. God created the world to be good (Genesis 1), as Wesley noted many times. Our bodies are good. They are precious gifts from God to be used as instruments of the soul. The ultimate Christian form of survival after death is the resurrection of the body, of re-embodiment in the final New Creation. There we will have new and improved senses—or something resembling them, but better, Wesley thought. He definitely was not against the sensory or physical world, just as he was not against money. But he warned against loving the useful inanimate world, mere things, property, and material wealth, more than we love conscious realities like God, other people, and animals. People and animals were created by God to be loved as final ends, not to be exploited as mere means to ends or purposes not their own. The end of the world will mean the end of worldliness.

The Means and Ends of Grace

Morality, spirituality, and their "proper objects" were Wesley's primary concerns and highest values. They involve inwardness, but they also make good use of what he called "externals" or sensory objects, processes, and actions. Good works are "externals" performed with our bodies. All Works of Mercy and Works of Piety are both good works and means of grace. External physical objects, inanimate things, and natural processes, may be legitimately used for practical, personal, moral, and spiritual purposes. When we act helpfully toward others, we physically feed the hungry, clothe the poor, house the homeless, heal the sick, give sight to the blind (as todays doctors can do), and so much else. All of these involve bodily actions and material resources. Properly used and valued, material things, processes, and physical activities are very good *as means* to much more desirable *ends* beyond themselves. The most "proper objects" of value are higher ends, final ends.

Wesley classified both Works of Mercy and Works of Piety as *means of grace*, not as final ends. These are the ways God has promised to meet us and be with us. The grace part has much more value than the means part, but both are essential. Christian ethics and moral acts of justice, love, mercy, and compassion are Works of Mercy. They benefit others. We often do not realize it, but in addition to being means of help and well-being to others, they are also means of grace to ourselves. All devotional practices or Works of Piety like prayer, meditation, searching the scriptures, and participating in the sacraments—are means of grace to ourselves and of help and benefits to others. The second love commandment authorizes us to love ourselves as well as others, but not in merely materialistic and selfish ways.

Wesley thought that the two protestant sacraments, Baptism and the Lord's Supper, involve both means and ends. Both are significant *means* of grace to even more significant spiritual *ends*, but these are very different. The proper *ends* of the sacraments are "internal," he insisted, but the physical *means* are "external." He accepted the ordinary definition of a "sacrament" as "an *outward* sign of *inward* grace, and a means whereby we receive the same."[8] He defined "means of grace," as "outward signs, words, or actions, ordained of God, and appointed for this end—to be the *ordinary* channels whereby He might convey to men, preventing, justifying, or sanctifying grace."[9]

In his sermon on "The Means of Grace," Wesley noted that both the Lord's Supper and Baptism use purely mind-less, physical, "external," material objects as means—wine (or grape juice), bread (or wafers), and water. There is no magic in any of these, he insisted. They are just ordinary objects of sense. The wine and bread are physical *signs or symbols* of the blood and body of Christ, *not literally* the blood and body of Christ—as in the Roman Catholic doctrine of transubstantiation. If they look, taste, smell, and feel like wine and bread, they really are wine and bread, not human blood and flesh, Wesley thought, because God gave us trustworthy senses.

There is no inherent magical power in the physical "elements" of the sacraments that will automatically make participants better persons. "Whosoever therefore imagines there is any intrinsic *power* in any means whatsoever does greatly err, not knowing the Scriptures, neither the power of God."[10] Merely taking part the sacraments *in the absence* of proper inward spiritual orientations, experiences, affections, efforts, structures, and goals will not do anyone any good. "We allow likewise that all outward means whatever, if separate from the Spirit of God, cannot profit at all, cannot conduce in any degree either to the knowledge or love of God . . . And all outward things, unless he work in them and by them, are mere weak and beggarly elements."[11] Did you ever take communion when "your heart was not in it," or "your head was not in it," and you only "went through the motions"? Your "head" and your "heart" should be attuned and engaged—as well as your body. The sacraments channel both "the knowledge [and] love of God."

God could turn *anything* into a sacramental object, a distinctive means of grace, Wesley thought. God can even bestow grace without using any external means at all: "We know likewise that he is able to give the same grace, though there were no means on the face of the earth. In this sense, we may affirm that with regard to God, there is no such thing as means, seeing he is equally able to work whatsoever pleaseth him by any or by none at all."[12]

Our historical situation as Christians, however, is that God has provided these sacraments to us "to be the ordinary channels whereby He might convey to men, preventing, justifying, or sanctifying grace."[13] (Wesley did not say so, but we might wonder if a loving God has not also provided other symbolical but effective means of grace to those in other religions and cultures.) All sacramental means of grace could have been otherwise, but water, bread, and wine were ordained *for us* given our own Christian history. We can acknowledge this without depreciating or denying what God has done for and given to others. Roman Catholics recognize many additional sacraments like confession and the last rites, and Wesley himself recognized many additional Works of Piety that are effective means of grace.

Wesley said of fasting as a means of grace, "It is not all; nor yet is it nothing. It is not the end; but it is a precious means thereto; a means which God himself has ordained, and in which therefore, when it is duly used, he will surely give us his blessing."[14] He would say the same thing about the physical elements of the sacraments. "God *can* give the end without any means at all; but you have no reason to think He *will*,[15] he warned; "Therefore constantly and carefully use all those means which he has appointed to be the ordinary channels of His grace. Use every means which either reason or Scripture recommends."[16] Of course, we know that what works for some people will not work for others, but most Christians are blessed who participate intensely in the sacraments and other Works of Piety.

Christians, Wesley thought, should not overvalue the external sacraments as final ends or think that the sacramental elements have any magical powers. They should not go the other extreme either and undervalue them as worthless or sinful, as did some of the Moravians, those who thought faith alone to be sufficient. They should be properly valued as historically contingent but generally effective means to the proper ends of religion. "Remember also, to use all means *as means*; as ordained, not for their own sake, but in order to the renewal of your soul in righteousness and true holiness. If, therefore, they actually tend to this, well; but, if not, they are dung and dross."[17] The sacramental elements and our bodily participation in them are nothing more than means to spiritual ends beyond themselves.

So what are the proper spiritual ends of the sacraments and other means of grace? Wesley's answer above was, "righteousness and true holiness." He further explained,

> But we allow that the whole value of the means depends on their actual subservience to the ends of religion; that, consequently all these means, when separated from the end, are less than nothing, and vanity; that if they do not actually conduce to the knowledge and love of God they are not acceptable in his sight; yea, rather, they are an abomination before him; a stink in his nostrils.[18]

Here "the knowledge and love of God" are added to "righteousness and true holiness" as proper ends of the means of grace. All of these ends—righteousness, holiness, the knowledge of God, the love of God—are internal to us. They exist only within our souls. They enrich and bless our souls. They are happenings, changes, efforts, sensitivities, affections, and insights within our personal consciousness. "Visible" external and physical sacramental objects are means to such "invisible" internal spiritual ends.

The "righteousness" part of this means that morally we "truly and earnestly repent of [our] sins, and are in love and charity with [our] neighbors, and intend to lead a new life, following the commandments of God, and walking from henceforth in his holy ways." Ideally, we come to the table *after* we have restored the moral balance between ourselves and anyone else we have offended or harmed, though sometimes we may only intend to do this *"henceforth."* This kind of moral balance involves restoring or recreating mutual union, trust, confidence, reconciliation, forgiveness, acceptance, and affection. It may also include repatriations or compensations. The "holiness" part means that we come together and commune in love for God and our neighbors, for holiness is love, Wesley thought. "Love" means that our whole hearts, our whole persons, are profoundly engaged affectively. The "knowledge" part means that the appropriate beliefs or mental "scripts" inform our minds.

Wesley elsewhere identified another end or goal of participating in God's "ordinances"—an increased *sensitivity to the presence of God* with and within us. The pure in heart, he said see God in his ordinances. Whether they appear in the great congregation to 'pay him the honor due unto his name, and worship him in the beauty of holiness' [Psalms 96:8-9], or 'enter into their closets' and there pour out their souls before their 'Father which is in secret' [Matthew 6:6]; whether they search the oracles of God, or hear the ambassadors of Christ proclaiming glad tidings of salvation; or by eating of that bread and drinking of that cup...In all these his appointed ways they find such a near approach as cannot be expressed.[19]

We have no adequate words to express what the sacraments do for us as means of grace, but some words, like Wesley's above, can help us to make some sense of them. Can you think of any other words that might help?

Final Ends

Choosing both the "best ends" and the "fittest means of attaining them" are very important, as Wesley indicated. Some desirable ends are more valuable than others. Some desirable ends serve as means to even better things beyond themselves. Some good things are even better than other good things. Some good things are final ends in and of themselves. But what?

If you are unemployed, your immediate goal is to get a job, but having a job is both directly rewarding in itself and a means to even more desirable ends beyond itself, like supporting yourself and your family, enjoying some of the comforts of life, and, if lucky, finding personal fulfillment in the work you do. But what are the *ultimate* goals, concerns, and values of work, play, and life?

The best answer ever given is implicit in the two love commandments of Jesus—loving God is our most ultimate or final end, and loving others as yourself—or as Christ has loved us—is second unto it. Loving God, our neighbors, and ourselves, (and every unique sentient creature God has made) are the most significant goals and purposes of life. Philosophers call the "proper objects" or final ends of love "intrinsic values,"—things inherently good that ought to be cherished for their own sakes. Unique conscious individuals, created or Uncreated, are final ends in themselves, valuable for their own sakes, and they are the most "proper objects" of our moral and spiritual concerns and devotions.

God is our ultimate and final end, *the ultimate end in himself*, Wesley taught. God should not be viewed or valued merely as a means to our personal ends. Instead, we should love God "for His own sake,"[20] and not just for what God can do for us, (as in the "prosperity gospel"). We should love God and use the world, not love the world and use God to enrich ourselves and improve our social status. The first love commandment identifies God as that unique reality having unsurpassable intrinsic worth, the one who truly deserves to be loved with all our hearts, souls, minds, and strength. To quote St. Anselm, "God is that being than whom none greater [better] can be conceived." In Wesley's own similar words, God is the one who "necessarily includes all good."[21] God has every conceivable perfect-making attribute essential for infinite intrinsic goodness, and this perfection *entitles* God to our ultimate love, contemplation, devotion, and service. God is worthy of it. God deserves it. God is good.

We and our neighbors, (including the animals), are intrinsically valuable but finite ends. As unique conscious individuals, we have immense worth in, to, and for ourselves, though secondary to God's infinite inherent goodness. Conscious individuals like ourselves ought to be cherished and loved for our own sakes, but why? Is it merely because we exemplify the four or five natural good-making image of God qualities we discussed earlier? Or is there more to it than that? Doesn't each unique person or animal have an additional and practically uncountable set of valuable qualities, capabilities, experiences, activities, and relations? Let's think about that.

Consider some unique person you greatly admire and love. Let's call this person your "friend," though she or he may be your spouse, child, parent, close relative, or acquaintance. Can your friend's total value and reality be completely understood in terms of nothing more than her or his four or five natural image of God qualities—being a spirit, a self-starter, with understanding, will (affections), and liberty of choice? Doesn't your unique friend have much more reality and much greater value than that? The full reality and value of any person includes embodiment, but for now let's consider only the soul or enduring consciousness of your friend. How many words would we have to use in order to capture *the total richness in goodness* of that?

Your friend's complete soul includes every particular thought he or she has ever had all the way through life, every particular sensory experience, every feeling, desire, emotion, affection, every voluntary effort, self-initiative, free choice, every intentional act, every aspect of his or her station in life and its duties, everything that makes her or him into the very definite, complete, unique, and valuable person she or he is.

Your friend's concrete personal *reality* far exceeds the few abstract image of God qualities shared with others. So does your friend's inherent *worth*. This is true of each one of us. Our image of God qualities *plus* everything else that describes us as inherently valuable individuals make up our full definiteness, uniqueness, and intrinsic goodness. Morally, all intrinsically valuable unique persons (and animals) in their entirety ought to be valued and treated as ends in themselves, and never merely as a means to someone else's ends or purposes not their own. Of course, others may "use" us without being immoral, but only if we concur or consent. And only thus may we "use" them.

Wesley never said that we as unique human individuals ought to be valued and loved for our own sakes as final ends—using just those words—though he did say something like that of God. Still, he obviously valued and loved us and himself in our full uniqueness and definiteness, and not just because we share the few image of God qualities we all have in common. Many of Wesley's words really do add up to this. He claimed, for example, that Christian happiness contains an intense awareness that God is "presiding over the whole universe as over a single person, so watching over every single person as if he were the whole universe."[22] Also, "One soul is of more value than all the world beside."[23] Individual souls have an infinite worth, not in themselves, but by virtue of their relationship with God, that is, because loves them: "Man is not only a house of clay, but an immortal spirit; a spirit made in the image of God, an incorruptible picture of the God of glory; a spirit of infinitely more value than the whole of earth; of more value than the sun, moon, and stars put together; yea than the whole material creation."[24] God loves and cares for us as individuals—like a good shepherd searching for one lost sheep.

At Aldersgate Wesley's "heart was strangely warmed." As he later described this experience, something also happened at Aldersgate to his "head." His "head" received and welcomed a very important new insight. He realized that everything he had been preaching to other people *applied to him*, to John Wesley, to the unique person that he was. As he put it, "I felt my heart strangely warmed. I felt I did trust in Christ, Christ alone, for salvation; and an assurance was given me that He had taken away my sins, even mine, and saved me from the law of sin and death."[25] He admitted later that he did not have that "assurance" constantly after Aldersgate, but that God loves *me*, and Christ gave his life for *me* (Wesley's italics, usually) are themes that appear many times in his sermons and writings—for example, "Christ loved *me*, and gave himself for *me*;"[26] and "This all-powerful, all wise, all-gracious Being, this Governor of all, loves me . . . And I love him."[27]

At Aldersgate, Wesley's heart was strangely warmed. There also he realized mentally that God loved and greatly valued *him*, the fully definite, concrete, and unique person that he was as John Wesley. He knew in both his head and his heart that God loved *him* in his fullness and uniqueness for his own sake, not just because of his generic humanity, and not just because of his four or five abstract image of God qualities. So it is with all of us.

Notes

1. Wesley, "An Israelite Indeed," *Works*, 3, 286.
2. Wesley, "A Plain Account of Christian Perfection," *The Works of the Reverend John Wesley, A.M.*, ed. John Emory, 6, 521.
3. Wesley, "Upon Our Lord's Sermon on the Mount, IX," *Works*, 1, 637.
4. Wesley, "The Way to the Kingdom," *Works*, 1, 226, italics added.
5. Wesley, "Original Sin," *Works*, 2, 179-180.
6. Wesley, "Wandering Thoughts," *Works*, 2, 127.
7. Wesley, "The Spirit of Bondage and Adoption," *Works*, 1, 253.
8. Wesley, "The Means of Grace," *Works*, 1, 381, italics added.
9. Ibid.
10. Ibid., 382.
11. Ibid.
12. Ibid.
13. Ibid.
14. Wesley, "Upon Our Lord's Sermon on the Mount, VII," *Works*, 1, 593-594.
15. Wesley, "The Means of Grace," *Works*, 1, 394.

16. Wesley, "The Nature of Enthusiasm," *Works,* 2, 59-60.
17. Ibid., *Works*, 1, 396-397.
18. Ibid., 381.
19. Wesley, "Upon Our Lord's Sermon on the Mount, III," *Works*, 1, 512.
20. Wesley, "Upon Our Lord's Sermon on the Mount, IX," *Works*, 1, 635.
21. Wesley, "Original Sin," *Works*, 2, 173.
22. Wesley, "A Plain Account of Genuine Christianity," Outler, 187.
23. Wesley, "On Family Religion," *Works*, 3, 337.
24. Wesley, "What is Man?" *Works*, 3, 460.
25. Wesley, "Journal, 24 May 24, 1738," *Works,* 18, 250.
26. Ibid., See also Wesley, "Original Sin," *Works*, 2, 184, italics his; Wesley, "What is Man?" *Works*, 3, 460-461, Wesley, "Spiritual Worship," *Works*, 3, 96, and in many other writings.
27. Wesley, "A Plain Account of Genuine Christianity," Outler, 187.

CHAPTER 10

WAS JESUS EVER HAPPY? ARE YOU?

Over the centuries, much attention has been given to Jesus as a "suffering servant," but the positive features of his inward constitution and the inherent value of his unique life in, to, and for himself have been neglected, especially the question of his happiness. This final chapter will explain how John Wesley can help us give an affirmative and intelligent answer to the question, "Was Jesus ever happy?" It will also help us to understand and pursue more successfully our own happiness or well-being.

The suffering of Jesus is often heavily emphasized, to the neglect of all the positive values, experiences, thoughts, affections, choices, and activities internal to and inherent within his unique life and inner personal conscious reality or soul. Without getting into current "historical Jesus" debates, we can safely assume that a relatively non-controversial and historically reliable understanding of what Jesus was like, i.e., of his general personality and character, may be abstracted from the four Gospels. What Jesus was actually like within himself has a significant bearing on whether or not he was ever happy. Even if the real historical Jesus turns out to be too elusive to pin down, we can still profit from examining and applying Wesley's understanding of "happiness" to ourselves.

What Did Wesley Mean by "Happiness"?

At least two different concepts of "happiness" are present in Western thought. Wesley affirmed one and rejected the other.

First, according to the *hedonic* view, happiness is *nothing more than* hav-

111

ing as much pleasure and as little pain as possible over an extended period of time. Pleasures themselves may differ *in quality*, some "higher" or "nobler" than others, as John Stuart Mill maintained,[1] and as Wesley earlier anticipated. Hedonic unhappiness consists *only* of prolonged pains and sufferings, whether "physical," that is, bodily localized, or "mental," that is, psychological.

Second, the *eudaimonistic* understanding of happiness, dating back to Aristotle, is pluralistic; it has more than one part. It includes pleasure *along with other* essential happiness-making qualities and relations. Happiness is a matter of actualizing both our universally human and our uniquely personal potentials for *many* desirable "good for us" qualities, activities, capacities, virtues, and relations. This kind of happiness is often called "well-being," "excellence," "fulfillment," "essence-actualization," "self-realization," etc. Actualizing pleasure is only one highly desirable "good for us" thing, but there are others.

Pleasure is a very good thing, a very fulfilling thing, but pleasure *alone* does not constitute our complete well-being or happiness. Many additional "good for us" human capacities, qualities, activities, and relationships are indispensable components of true happiness—things like personal growth, knowing, thinking, responsible choosing, diverse feelings and emotions, conscience and faithfulness to it, physical and mental activities, diverse adventures, sensory stimulation, desire satisfaction, and virtuous moral motives, dispositions, and actions. *Such things do not produce our happiness or well-being; their actualization is our happiness or well-being.* All are typically accompanied by their own distinctive qualities of pleasure, but their positive happiness-value is far more than merely being sources of enjoyment.

Eudaimonistic unhappiness includes but does not consist solely in prolonged pain and suffering. Additionally, it involves the loss, lack, or *absence* of many fulfilling "good for us" properties, and in the actualization of their contraries, that is, in the *presence* of ignorance, confusion, falsehood, evildoing, and miserable immoral dispositions, feelings, and "affections" or "tempers" as Wesley called them.

Wesley himself identified our well-being or happiness with our redeemed, restored, image of God potentials, as uniquely actualized in our full definiteness as individuals. He wrote of "attaining all the image of God" and "advancing the image of God in us."[2] This involves lifelong growth or sanctification in spiritual and moral beliefs, experiences, motives, sensitivities, dispositions, and behaviors—all indispensable components of genuine human happiness or well-being. Each of us can fulfill our desirable Godlike potentials only in our own unique and distinctive ways, so being true to our individuality is just as important as being true to our common image of God qualities. Wesley's understanding of human happiness or well-being was eudaimonistic.[3] Happiness consists of actualizing our image of God capacities, especially love, in our own personal and definite ways.

In this discussion, "Was Jesus ever happy?" will be about Wesley eudaimonistic kind of abundant living.

A Wesleyan Argument for the Happiness of Jesus

Wesley *did not in fact* ask or answer, "Was Jesus ever happy?" What follows will show how Wesley *could have* affirmed that Jesus was a *"happy* servant" for much of his life—in addition to being at times a *"suffering* servant," a "man of sorrows, acquainted with grief."

The main argument runs as follows:

1. The principle ingredients of genuine human happiness, as John Wesley *correctly* identified them, are: a. love and obedience to the love commandments; b. spiritual beliefs, knowledge, experiences, dispositions, virtues, sensitivities, and activities; c. moral beliefs, knowledge, experiences, dispositions, virtues, sensitivities, and activities, d. pleasures; enjoyments, joy, and e. freedom from as much pain, suffering, unhappiness, and loss as humanly possible. This is not the whole story, but it will suffice for now.

2. Anyone who exemplifies these definitional components of happiness or well-being is indeed truly happy, at least to the extent and duration that these are present.

3. Jesus momentously exemplified all of these components of happiness for most of his life, even if not during his passion and crucifixion.

4. Conclusion: Jesus was truly happy for most of his life.

The third point here makes no direct appeal to controversial historical specifics about Jesus. Rather, it assumes only that the four Gospels give us an accurate general knowledge of the overall *character* of Jesus during his life, ministry, and death. A commonsense understanding of human nature itself also supports some of the following applications to Jesus.

In more detail, for Wesley, genuine human happiness or well-being consists at least in the following (and perhaps more).

Love and Obedience to the Love Commandments

Wesley thought that the most basic component of human happiness is living in loving obedience to Jesus' two love commandments. Without love, no one can be happy, he insisted,[4] and "according to the degree of or love is the degree of our happiness."[5] Christians are happy and joyful people because they are loving people.[6] (We might want to add that non-Christians who are loving people are also happy and joyful. Christians have no monopoly on love.) Genuine happiness consists in loving God and our neighbors, but definitely not in loving the mindless things of the world over all else, as do worldly people, and definitely not in loving ideas, beliefs, doctrines, and truths above all else, as do dogmatists and many intellectuals.

People can love the wrong things. Most do, Wesley thought. He explained, "To bless men; to make men happy, was the great business for which our Lord came into the world. . . . Knowing that happiness is our common aim, and that an innate instinct continually urges us to the pursuit of it, he in the kindest manner applies to that instinct, and directs it to its proper object. Though all men desire, yet few attain, happiness, because they seek it where it is not to be found."[7] This actually sounds more like Aristotle than Jesus, but Wesley may have thought that this is what Jesus meant by living "more abundantly" (John 10:10). Wesley himself usually talked about happiness.

Real happiness depends as much on *who and what* we love as on *that* we love, but all who love God, other people, and animals are happy people, Wesley thought. (Strictly speaking, this list should include "every creature that God has made"—to the neglect of none.) As Wesley indicated, next to the love of God, loving our neighbor "affords the greatest happiness of which we are capable."[8] Loving others is both fulfilling and enjoyable to ourselves; it is also helpful and beneficial to others. Wesley wrote about "The joy of loving, or of being loved"[9] and "the pleasure of loving."[10]

In addition, love *fulfills* the most important features of the image of God within us. Wesley had a very rich understanding of our "natural" image of God capacities. We are (1) *spirits* (immaterial souls) with (2) *understanding*, (3) *will* (desires, feelings, affections), and (4) *liberty* (free choice).[11] Love falls under "will" as our most important image of God quality.

What theologian of consequence prior to Wesley, if any, ever affirmed that *love is the image of God within us*? (Almost all said it is "Reason.") Wesley wrote, "But love is the very image of God: it is the brightness of his glory. By love man is not only made like God, but in some sense one with him."[12] Through love, we fully identify with God, and God fully identifies with us. Thus, we are one with him. "Above all," he wrote, "remembering that God is love, he [the Christian] is conformed to the same likeness. He is full of love to his neighbor: of universal love. . . ."[13]

As for the Jesus of the Gospels, would it really be too presumptuous to think that he was an intensely, constantly, and consistently loving person? He actually exemplified all the above image of God qualities in his own distinctive ways. He was an embodied spirit. He was capable of understanding. He increased in knowledge and wisdom. He had a will—all the normal desires, emotions, dispositions, affections, and feelings that human beings usually have. He exercised responsible liberty or freedom of choice. Most importantly, Jesus was a loving and caring person. He was love incarnate.

Wesley thought that the "faith that works through love," as St. Paul put it, fulfills both human nature and God's "moral" image, as well as the law, the two love commandments. Said Wesley, "Thou O man of God, stand fast in love, in the image of God wherein thou art made."[14] The two love commandments are rock-bottom Christianity, Methodism, and "true religion."[15] The Jesus of the four Gospels actually lived by and fulfilled the love commandments. He loved God most of all, himself as he loved others, and others as he loved himself. We have no good "historical" reasons for thinking otherwise. If so, as an intensely, constantly, consistently, and actively loving person, Jesus was indeed an intensely, constantly, consistently, and actively happy person. Thus, Wesley could have affirmed that Jesus was indeed a happily loving person, but there is still more. Before moving on, ask yourself, "Am I a happy, joyful, fulfilled, and actively loving person?"

Spiritual Beliefs, Knowledge, Experiences, Dispositions, Virtues, and Activities

Without being naïve about the evils that befall us, Wesley was convinced that profoundly religious people are generally happy, and unreligious people are generally unhappy. Toward the end of his sermon on "The Important Question," after much discussion Wesley concluded, "It has been proved . . . that religion is happiness, that wickedness is misery."[16] He rejected the idea that Christians must be miserable in this world so they can be happy in the next. The real options, he argued, are between unhappiness both here and hereafter, and happiness both here and hereafter. The "Important Question" is: "Will you be happy here and hereafter—in the world that now is, and in that which is to come? Or will you be miserable here and hereafter in time and in eternity?"[17]

Wesley advised, "Singly aim at God . . . Pursue one thing: happiness in knowing, in loving, in serving God."[18] Further, "But true religion, or a heart right toward God and man, implies happiness as well as holiness."[19] Real Methodists are "happy in God, yea always happy."[20] Christians are more likely to live a happy life than non-Christians because spirituality is an essential happiness-making, fulfilling, and pleasure-giving property. Christians take "pleasure in God."[21]

Enduring happiness, Wesley argued, partly involves "the pleasures of religion," specifically, pleasures derived from "the love of God, and of all mankind," and from the more enduring joy, delight, comfort, peace, gratitude, and rejoicing that such love brings.[22] He regarded such pleasures as much more lasting and deeply satisfying and fulfilling than the fleeting pleasures of imagination and sensation. He called them "nobler enjoyments" because they are qualitatively superior to "low" sensory pleasures.[23]

The Jesus of the Gospels was unquestionably a profoundly spiritual or religious person. He was intensely open and attuned to God and obedient to God's loving will. He completely identified himself with God, and God completely identified himself with Jesus. "I and my father are one," he said (John 10:30). He was truly "God-intoxicated." He found both personal fulfillment and enjoyment in his own spiritual beliefs, knowledge, experiences, dispositions, sensitivities, virtues, and practices. The spiritual image of God was present in Jesus. Wesley could have concluded that Jesus was a profoundly happy person because he was profoundly spiritual in all such ways. Pause once more to consider whether you are joyful and fulfilled *because* you are a profoundly spiritual person.

Moral Beliefs, Knowledge, Experiences, Dispositions, Virtues, Sensitivities, and Activities

Morality was never totally separated from spirituality in Wesley's mind, but there is more to morality than love alone. Love to God and all humankind is the "one, single ground" of all moral virtues;[24] it is their source or fount. But there are additional moral virtues, and actualizing and acting upon them is essential to image-of-God-fulfillment-happiness, pleasure-happiness, and unique self-actualization happiness.

The *moral imitation* of God (and Jesus) looms large in Wesley's Christian ethics. The Christian "knows the most acceptable worship of God is to imitate him he worships, so he is continually laboring to transcribe into himself all his imitable perfections: in particular, his justice, mercy and truth, so eminently displayed in all his creatures."[25] God works, and we "labour" together with God to actualize our own moral and spiritual virtues. We *strive* for all Christian perfections, for sanctification, for holiness, for virtue, even if we succeed only by degrees, and then only with God's grace and help. In many writings, Wesley offered long lists of the Christian moral virtues that spring from love, but consider this one.

> And this universal, disinterested love is productive of all right affections. It is fruitful of gentleness, tenderness, sweetness; of humanity, courtesy and affability. It makes a Christian rejoice in the virtues of all, and bear a part in their happiness at the same time that he sympathizes with their pains and compassionates their infirmities. It creates modesty, condescension, prudence—together with calmness and evenness of temper. It is the parent of generosity, openness and frankness, void of jealousy and suspicion. It begets candor and willingness to believe and hope whatever is kind and friendly of every man, and invincible patience, never overcome of evil, but overcoming evil with good . . . The same love is productive of all right actions . . . It constrains him to do all possible good, of every possible kind, to all men; and makes him invariably resolved in every circum-

stance of life to do that, and that only, to others, which supposing he were himself in the same situation, he would desire they should do to him.[26]

As for the relevance of "doing good" and "being good" to happiness, Methodists think "that there is an inseparable connection between virtue and happiness; that none but a virtuous (or, as they usually express it, a religious) man can be happy."[27] Virtuous living is very enjoyable, as well as both personal and image-of-God-fulfilling. "Now if the doing good [gives] so much pleasure to one who acted merely from natural generosity, how much more must it give to one who does it on a nobler principle, the joint love of God and his neighbor? It remains, that the doing all which religion requires will not lessen, but immensely increase our happiness."[28] Once again, it "affords the greatest happiness of which we are capable."[29]

Applied to the Jesus of the Gospels, Wesley's account of the many moral virtues that flow from love seems to describe accurately his general character and behavior. The moral image of God was present in Jesus. He highly, perhaps perfectly, exemplified all the moral virtues, and this is further evidence that he was a profoundly happy person—both fulfilled and joyful. Wesley could have argued that because of his exemplary ethical beliefs, virtues, motives, dispositions, sensitivities, and deeds, Jesus had "all the happiness of which [he was] capable." Once again, pause for a moment to ask yourself, "Am I developing myself, being true to myself, and finding joy and fulfillment in living a virtuous Christian life, both internally and externally?"

Pleasures, Enjoyments, Joy

Wesley thought that Christians have a much better chance than non-Christians of achieving image of God essence fulfillment, uniqueness fulfillment, and hedonic enjoyment, both here and hereafter. God gives no absolute guarantees, but God's odds are better. Wesley was definitely not against "the pursuit of happiness." He did not use this exact phrase, but he did write of "they that pursue happiness,"[30] and of "Pursuing happiness, but never overtaking it."[31] Wesley was all for happiness, understood as partly composed of pleasures, but not of pleasures alone. He repeatedly affirmed the goodness and desirability of pleasure as such.

He wrote, "We no more affirm pleasure in general to be unlawful than eating and drinking."[32] But, he thought, most people go about pursuing pleasure in the wrong way, "never overtaking it." Worldly people live mainly to experience the external world and its sensory pleasures. They live only (or mainly) for worldly sensory pleasures. Many intellectuals live mainly for mental pleasures. Because they, too, most love the wrong things, they do not enjoy and are not enriched by grace, faith, spirituality, love, the moral virtues, and works of mercy and grace. To this theme Wesley gave much attention.[33]

Wesley vigorously defended the importance of pleasure, but not exclusively or primarily the sensory pleasures of the world. He objected to the pursuit of "low," worldly, sensual pleasures because they are fleeting, transient, disappointing, and ultimately unsatisfying and unfulfilling. He said, "You cannot find your long-sought happiness in all the pleasures of the world . . . which may amuse, but cannot satisfy."[34] Wesley did not say so, but another very serious problem with loving "mere things" is that they cannot love us back. They do not fulfill the inherently social aspects of our human and personal natures.

At times, Wesley may have underestimated the positive contributions of sensory enjoyments to a Christian's, or anyone else's, genuine happiness. After all, our senses and their experienced objects were also created for us by God (Proverbs 20:12), as was sensory pleasure itself. Wesley's most serious objection was actually to futile efforts to enjoy the things of the world without God, or in the absence of God, i.e., without a spiritual awareness of God's presence in sensory objects and processes, and while being oblivious to what God expects of us regarding inanimate things.

Wesley did not object to enjoying the world under or within God. Any Christian, he wrote, "may smell a flower, or eat a bunch of grapes, or take any other pleasure which does not lessen but increase his delight in God."[35] Again, "The man who loves God feels that 'God hath given him all things richly to enjoy.' He delights in his works, and surveys with joy all the creatures which God hath made. Love increases both the number of his delights, and the weight of them, a thousandfold. For in every creature he sees as in a glass the glory of the great Creator."[36]

Few people have seriously considered pleasures within the life and experiences of Jesus. We have many words for experiencing pleasure—

enjoyment, joy, having fun, etc. The Gospels may have neglected this, but *we* can ask: Did Jesus ever have any fun? Did he ever enjoy anything? Human nature itself actually provides us with a good answer. If Jesus was as "fully human" as orthodoxy insists, surely he did have a lot of fun. Jesus regularly experienced all the ordinary joys and pleasures of exuberant and vibrant human living. He enjoyed eating, drinking, and dining with outcasts and sinners. Perhaps he enjoyed defying the strict religious purity conventions of his day. As fully human, he had both mundane and sublime goals, and he achieved many of them. Through almost all of this, he enjoyed life and found personal fulfillment in it.

Most of us enjoy and find great personal fulfillment in loving and helping others, as well as in identifying intensely with and serving God. Surely Jesus did as well. Wesley was convinced that the key elements that *define* human happiness—love, spirituality, and morality—are pleasant, image-of-God-fulfilling, and uniquely self-actualizing. Jesus had innumerable enjoyable, fulfilling, and intense identification and service experiences over the course of his lifetime. As fully human, Jesus experienced all of the normal interests, desires, emotions, feelings, responsibilities, and activities that we all experience, as well as their satisfactions and their frustrations. As Wesley indicated, "Our blessed Lord himself had a will as a man; otherwise he had not been a man."[37] On Wesleyan grounds, we can affirm that Jesus himself found abundant image-of-God-fulfillment, much delight or pleasure, and much self-actualization in doing what Jesus would do, thinking what Jesus would think, choosing what Jesus would choose, willing what Jesus would will, feeling what Jesus would feel, and loving who, what, and how Jesus would love.

Before going further, pause once again and ask yourself, "Do I enjoy living like Jesus in all such ways?"

Freedom from as Much Pain, Suffering, Loss, and Unhappiness as Humanly Possible

Wesley was convinced that a moral and spiritual life is, on the whole, a happy life, but this does not mean that it contains no pain, suffering, or unhappiness. Christian happiness is never pure or unmitigated bliss; it is always mixed with pain and suffering. Wesley identified at least two ways in which good, moral, spiritual, loving people are likely to suffer, no matter what. He definitely did not believe that being a Christian will deliver us from all ills.

First, suffering, accidents, diseases, poverty, losses, and malicious deeds by wicked persons do afflict good people.[38] Wesley was not naïve enough to think that being a Christian, a Methodist, or a loving person guarantees protection from all losses, temptations, harms, accidents, diseases, poverty, pain, suffering, and unhappiness. He did not preach a guaranteed-prosperity gospel. As he recognized, a Christian "may accidentally suffer loss, poverty, pain; but in all these things he is more than conqueror."[39] Still, the saint has a much better chance of being happy than the sinner.

Second, even the life of love involves some inherent suffering. Wesley acknowledged that loving people may suffer precisely because they are loving people. Christians do deny themselves and carry crosses.[40] He defined a "cross," as "anything contrary to our will, anything displeasing to our nature."[41] Overcoming worldliness (sacrificing or dethroning worldly desires and pleasures, delaying gratification, controlling our passions) is contrary to our unredeemed and untamed natural will. Actually doing so can be very distressing, thus displeasing, to some aspects of our basic human nature, at least temporarily.

More importantly, Wesley recognized with St. Paul that loving people are compassionate, which means that they bear one another's burdens and suffer with those who suffer, while also rejoicing with those who rejoice. Suffering is an integral part of the very definition of "compassion." A Christian will "rejoice in the virtues of all, and bear a part in their happiness at the same time that he sympathizes with their pains and compassionates their infirmities."[42] "Sympathizing sorrow," includes pains of soul, but "These are 'tears that delight and sighs that waft to heaven.'"[43] The sufferings involved in compassion are profoundly fulfilling and joyful. Through the best and worst of times, the Christian "has learned to be content, to be easy, thankful, joyful, happy."[44]

Christians really do carry crosses, bear one another's burdens, console one another, suffer with those who suffer, and act to relieve and prevent unnecessary suffering and loss. They also have the inner "courage to be" (as Paul Tillich called it), and the strength to endure such things. Like Christ, Christians (and all loving people living up to the best light they have) are suffering servants. Yet, even in that, they find great and enduring happiness—both fulfillment and joy—"tears that delight." The pleasures associated with compassion, love, gratitude, just dealings, and other virtues are not always absolutely pure. They are often mixed with pains of soul, but even these are integral parts of fulfillment-happiness and actualizing God's image within us, for God suffers with those who suffer. Writing of "the Lord Jehovah," Wesley proclaimed, "Trust in him who suffered a thousand times more than ever you can suffer. Hath he not all power in heaven and earth?"[45] Wesley's God was "patripassianate." God has real feelings, suffering included.

Wesley argued that loving people do avoid certain kinds of suffering and pains of soul. They are spared the inherent misery and uneasiness that is normally a part of immoral vices, feelings, dispositions, and deeds. Moral vices or "vile affections" are inherently miserable, he contended. "All unholy tempers are unhappy tempers. Ambition, covetousness, vanity, inordinate affection, malice, revengefulness, carry their own punishment with them, and avenge themselves on the soul wherein they dwell."[46] In this sense, vice is its own punishment.

Wesley developed this theme in many ways and in many writings. He identified all of the following as miserable vices: anger, fretfulness, vengeance, ill-will, malice, hatred, jealousy, envy, and "any other temper opposite to kindness."[47] He may have underestimated the perverse but mixed-with-pain pleasures that can attend such vices. Can you remember times when you were possessed or obsessed by any of these negative passions or feelings? Were you ever overwhelmed by guilt, seething with anger or hatred, obsessed by envy, or consumed by vengefulness (otherwise known as retributive justice, an eye for an eye)? If so, were you really happy then?

Wesley often explained how true religion brings many good things. It offers peace of soul that passes all understanding, assurance of God's love and acceptance, an inner experience of God's constant presence, a good and clear conscience toward and before God, a profound sense of forgiveness, reconciliation, and relief from guilt, escape from hopelessness and despair, and exemption from a great host of irrational fears, spiritual distresses, and existential anxieties. Being right with God gives us an abundant life as well as the strength and courage to be, to do, to love, to endure, and to persevere.[48]

Yes, the Jesus of the Gospels suffered compassionately with those who suffer, wept for and with those who weep, and bore the weight of our burdens and sins. He was indeed a suffering servant. He internalized and responded with unfathomable sensitivity and compassion to every sinner and sufferer, and to every pain, harm, loss, and tragedy. If God as represented by Jesus was (and is) hurt every time anyone else is hurt, then he bears or carries within himself all the heavy burdens of the world.

Jesus definitely endured the agonies of his own passion and crucifixion, and he felt abandoned by God at the end. Yet, for most of his life, in his innocence and confidence in God, he was free from the miseries and unpleasant "tempers" of the moral vices. He had his own peace of soul that passed all understanding. He did not live in guilt, hopelessness, anger, hatred, resentment, and despair. He lived with his own assurance of God's presence, love, and acceptance. He had a good and clear conscience before God. He was guilt free, and he was spared a great multitude of spiritual fears and existential disquietudes. He had the strength and courage to be, to do, to love, to endure, to persevere. Since he identified intensely if not completely with God, God was very real to him, and there was no hideous "God-shaped void" in his consciousness—except perhaps at the very of his life when he felt that God had forsaken him.

In sum, with John Wesley's help, we can now understand both that and how the Jesus of the Gospels was a very happy person for much if not most of his life. He actualized or fulfilled his own image of God potentials in his own unique way. Within himself, he was profoundly loving, spiritual, moral, and joyful. He was filled with delight in all of creation, and free from the despairs and miseries of sinful dispositions and deeds. Anyone who is like him, who lives in imitation of him, would be *fulfilled* in both their humanity and their personal individuality. And they would be *filled* with *joy* unspeakable. Anyone like him, anyone who is Christlike, would have a meaningful, happy, fulfilled, and abundant life. Do you?

Notes

1. See Rem B. Edwards, *Pleasures and Pains: A Theory of Qualitative Hedonism* (Ithaca: Cornell University Press, 1979).

2. Wesley, "Satan's Devices," *Works*, 2, 143.

3. An expanded case for Wesley's eudaimonistic understanding of "happiness" is found in Rem B. Edwards, *John Wesley's Values—And Ours* (Lexington, KY: Emeth, 2013), 244-246.

4. Wesley, "On Love," *Works*, 4, 386.

5. Wesley, "An Israelite Indeed," *Works*, 3, 283.

6. Wesley, "The Way to the Kingdom," *Works*, 1, 223-224.

7. Wesley, *Explanatory Notes on the New Testament*, comment on Matthew 5:2.

8. Wesley, "The Important Question," *Works*, 3, 189.

9. Ibid.

10. John Wesley, "A Plain Account of Genuine Christianity," Outler, 185.

11. Wesley, "The General Deliverance," *Works*, 2, 438-439. These features of the image of God are also discussed elsewhere, for example, Wesley, "The End of Christ's Coming," *Works*, 2, 474-475; Wesley, "The Good Steward," *Works*, 2, 284-285; Wesley, "On the Fall of Man," *Works*, 2, 409-410; Wesley, "The New Birth," *Works*, 2, 188.

12. Wesley, "The One Thing Needful," *Works*, 4, 355. See also "The Righteousness of Faith," *Works*, 1, 205.

13. Wesley, "A Plain Account of Genuine Christianity," Outler, 184.

14. Wesley, "The Righteousness of Faith," *Works*, 1, 205.

15. Wesley, "A Plain Account of Genuine Christianity," Outler, 184-185; Wesley, "The Character of a Methodist," *Works*, 9, 35, 37-38; Wesley, "The Way to the Kingdom," *Works*, 1, 221-224.

16. Wesley, "The Important Question," *Works*, 3, 197.

17. Ibid., 3, 197.

18. Wesley, "On Dissipation," *Works*, 3, 123.

19. Wesley, "The Way to the Kingdom," *Works*, 1, 223.

20. Wesley, "The Character of a Methodist," *Works*, 9, 35.

21. Wesley, "The More Excellent Way," *Works*, 3, 265.

22. Wesley, "The Important Question," *Works*, 3, 185.

23. Wesley, "A Plain Account of Genuine Christianity," Outler, 186; Wesley, "Spiritual Idolatry," *Works*, 3, 106; Wesley, "Original Sin," *Works*, 2, 180.

24. Wesley, "To the Inhabitants of Ireland," *Works*, 9, 284.

25. Wesley, "A Plain Account of Genuine Christianity," Outler, 184.

26. Ibid., 185.

27. Wesley, "To the Inhabitants of Ireland," *Works*, 9, 283.

28. Wesley, "The Important Question," 3, *Works*, 3, 191.

29. Ibid., 189.

30. Wesley, "On Mourning for the Dead," *Works*, 4, 239.
31. Wesley, "Spiritual Idolatry," *Works*, 3, 100.
32. Wesley, "Letter to Mr. Fleury," *Works*, 9, 393.
33. See Edwards, *John Wesley's Values—And Ours,* 90-104.
34. Wesley, "Spiritual Worship," *Works*, 3, 101.
35. Wesley, "The Reformation of Manners," *Works*, 2:318.
36. Wesley, "The Love of God," *Works*, 4, 343.
37. Wesley, "The Repentance of Believers," *Works*, 1, 337.
38. Wesley, "Death and Deliverance," *Works*, 4, 208-209; Wesley, "Heaviness through Manifold Temptations," *Works*, 2, 222-235.
39. Wesley, "The Important Question," *Works*, 3, 191.
40. Wesley, "Self-Denial," *Works*, 2, 238-252.
41. Ibid., 2, 243.
42. Wesley, "A Plain Account of Genuine Christianity," Outler, 185.
43. Wesley, "The Important Question," *Works*, 3, 191-192.
44. Wesley, "A Plain Account of Genuine Christianity," Outler, 186.
45. Wesley, "Heavenly Treasure in Earthen Vessels," *Works*, 4, 167.
46. Wesley, "The Important Question," *Works*, 3, 194.
47. Wesley, "On Love," *Works*, 4, 386; Wesley, "The New Birth," *Works*, 2, 195-196.
48. All of these themes are much further developed in Edwards, *John Wesley's Values—And Ours.*

About the Author

REM B. EDWARDS, Ph.D., grew up in the small town of Crawfordville, GA. He attended Emory at Oxford, then graduated in 1956 as a Philosophy major from Emory University in Atlanta with an A.B. degree. There he was elected to Phi Beta Kappa. Throughout graduate school, he was a Danforth Graduate Fellow, which paid for his entire graduate education. He received a B.D. degree from Yale University Divinity School (YDS) in 1959 and a Ph.D. in Philosophy from Emory University in 1962, where he studied under Charles Hartshorne. While at YDS he was the summer minister for the Old Brick Church Congregational in Clarendon, VT, and after completing YDS he served for a year as minister of Dixie Methodist Church in LaGrange, GA. After receiving his Ph.D. from Emory, he taught for four years at Jacksonville University in Florida, moved from there to the University of Tennessee in 1966, and retired from there partly in 1997 and partly in 1998. He kept an office on the University campus until the end of May, 2000. He was a U. T. Chancellor's Research Scholar in 1985 and a distinguished Lindsay Young Professor from 1987 through 1998. He continues to be professionally active.

His areas of specialization are the Philosophy of Religion, American Philosophy, Ethical Theory, Medical Ethics with a special focus on Mental Health Care Ethics, Ethics and Animals, and Formal Axiology. In recent years he has done considerable work on John Wesley.

Counting this one, he has published twenty two books. Those most relevant to religious readers are: *Reason and Religion* (New York: Harcourt, 1972, Lanham, MD: University Press of America, 1979, and Eugene, OR: Wipf & Stock, 2016); *Dialogues on Values and Centers of Value* (Amsterdam - New York: Rodopi, 2001), co-authored with Thomas M. Dicken; and *What Caused the Big Bang?* (Amsterdam - New York: Rodopi, 2001). *What Caused the Big Bang* received the "Best Book of 2001" award from the Editors of the Value Inquiry Book Series. Published by Emeth Press in 2012 were *John Wesley's Values—And Ours,* and *Spiritual Values and Evaluations.* Process Century Press published his *An Axiological Process Ethics* in 2013. Edwards has also published over a hundred articles and reviews. Three of his most recent articles are: "John Wesley's Non-Literal Literalism," *Wesleyan Theological Journal,* Fall, 2016; "Was Jesus Ever Happy? How John Wesley Could Have Answered," *Wesleyan Theological Journal,* Fall, 2017; and "A Genuine Monotheism for Christians, Muslims, Jews, and All," *Journal of Ecumenical Studies,* Fall, 2017.

He was an Associate Editor with the Value Inquiry Book Series, published by Rodopi, and responsible for books in Hartman Institute Axiological Studies special series. For a number of years he was also co-editor of the Advances in Bioethics book series published by JAI Press. In 2008, he became the founder and senior editor of the *Journal of Formal Axiology: Theory and Practice.*

Edwards was the President of the Tennessee Philosophical Association (1973-74), the Society for Philosophy of Religion (1981-82), and the Southern Society for Philosophy and Psychology, (1984-85). He is a Charter Member and Fellow of the Robert S. Hartman Institute for Formal and Applied Axiology, served on its Board of Directors from 1987 to 2013, and continues as an Emeritus member thereafter. In 1989 he became its Secretary/Treasurer, in 2007 its Secretary, and served until 2009. He is a lifelong Methodist.

www.ingramcontent.com/pod-product-compliance
Lightning Source LLC
Chambersburg PA
CBHW060838190426
43197CB00040B/2673